# POLITICS IN CZECHOSLOVAKIA, 1945-1971

J. F. N. Bradley
University of Manchester

UNIVERSITY
PRESS OF
AMERICA

Copyright © 1981 by
**University Press of America,Inc.'"**
P.O. Box 19101, Washington, D.C. 20036

Printed in the United States of America

Library of Congress Cataloging in Publication Data

Bradley, J. F. N. (John Francis Nejez), 1930-
    Politics in Czechoslovakia, 1945-1971.

    Bibliography: p.
    1. Czechoslovakia--Politics and government--
1945-    .  I. Title.
DB2218.7.B7      320.9437      80-5632
ISBN 0-8191-1582-7              AACR2
ISBN 0-8191-1583-5 (pbk.)

# CONTENTS

# PREFACE

When in 1968 the Department of Government introduced
a third year course, Comparative Communist Government, and the Czechoslovak model became its
component, it became evident that there were no
textbooks in English which we could recommend to
our students. Professor Taborsky's Communism in
Czechoslovakia 1948-1960 (Princeton, 1961)
concentrated on Communist personalities and policies
and was therefore of limited value. Profesor Ulc's
Politics in Czechoslovakia (San Francisco, 1970)
was a bare outline which included the reform movement in 1968 and its collapse, but necessarily
hardly touched on the institutional aspects of the
political system in Czechoslovakia which we
required for our course. Rather hurriedly I
prepared for our students a historical introduction,
Czechoslovakia: A Short History (Edinburgh, 1971);
however, by then the Social Science Research
Council offered to sponsor and finance a research
project on Communist governments, and Czechoslovakia
was one of the countries included in it.

With the research grant from the SSRC it was
possible to go to Czechoslovakia in search of
materials and collect them on the spot, because at
this stage Dubcek's Communist state threw open its
gates to Western political scientists and
researchers. Research material was located,
sometimes xeroxed, microfilmed or brought outright
to England. These accumulated sources, as well as
the new books published by the reformers in
Czechoslovakia, made it possible to tackle the
institutional problems of the political model,
expecially since they were no longer secret.
Czechoslovak Communist scientists could also be
consulted; in addition the research project
offered the benefit of sharing research findings
with British colleagues, who were simultaneously
working on similar problems in Poland and Jugoslavia. The result is this 'basic research text-
book'. The study outlines the unique democratic
model of government prior to the Communist coup

iv

d'état in 1948 and then examines the Communist
transformation of this system during the Stalinist
period and thereafter. After subjecting to
analysis the changing role of the Communist Party
within the system between 1948-1968, it becomes
clear that even the Communist Party found the
political model unworkable in Czechoslovak
conditions and tried to return to the system of
government as it existed prior to its seizure of
power in 1948. In 1968 it proposed to re-adopt a
multi-party system with free plural parliamentary
elections, thus strengthening parliament, weakening
central government, boosting up local government
and the judiciary, abolishing the power monopoly
of the Communist Party and practically dissolving
the security police (statni bezpecnost - which is
the Czechoslovak equivalent of the Soviet KGB).
However, the invasion of 1968 and the occupation of
Czechoslovakia by the Soviet Army and some other
armies of the Warsaw Pact, put a stop to these
attempts at re-establishing the status quo ante,
and resulted instead in the new federal system which
under the leadership of Dr Gustav Husak, Secretary
General of the Czechoslovak Communist Party and
Dubcek's successor, gradually tranformed itself
into the Soviet-type Communist model with only a
few specific Czechoslovak features.

I wish to put on record my gratitude to the
Social Science Research Council for its support;
numerous Czechoslovak political scientists, who
are still living in Czechoslovakia and therefore
must remain anonymous, for their help in collecting
research materials and taking them out of the
country. For helpful comments I am indebted to
Professor Radko Jansky of the University of St Louis
and, for his encouragement, to Professor Geraint
Parry of Manchester University.

John Bradley
July 1980

# CHAPTER I

## Provisional System 1945-48

### War and Liberation

In 1945 Czechoslovakia emerged from the war more
confused and disorganised than devasted. During
the war in Bohemia only some 3,014 buildings were
destroyed and some 10,000 damaged. While material
losses were heavier in Moravia (some 11,862
buildings destroyed and 19,000 damaged) Slovakia
suffered damage only in 1944, after the Slovak
uprising, when some sixty villages had been burnt
and destroyed. In addition Slovakia was heavily
damaged during the fighting between the Wehrmacht
and the Red Army, but this destruction lasted only
some six months. In any case, compared to the
devastation in Poland, the USSR or Germany, Czechoslovakia's was only a minor.

What caused disorganisation were the heavy
casualties inflicted on the Czechs and Slovaks in
a highly selective way by the Germans. Overall
losses were relatively minor: between September
1939 and May 1945 Czechoslovakia lost between
245,000 and 250,000 men, women and children. The
war left behind between 100,000 and 127,816 cripples.
Seventy-five thousand were executed and the
Communist Party of Czechoslovakia alone lost
24,920 members, of whom 3,649 were executed and
5,687 died in concentration camps. However, what
was most important about these losses was that
they affected the intelligentsia, traditionally a
group of people in charge of the political system
and the economy in Czechoslovakia. Moreover,
great population changes and movements increased
the confusion and disorganisation of the leaderless
people. Only in 1942 some 75,000 specialised
workers were transported to Germany as forced
labour; in 1943-4, 32,000 more followed them and
countless other workers were shipped to Austria to
build fortifications against the advancing Red

1

Army. Economically the Germans disorganised
Czechoslovakia as best they could; some 500,000
hectares of agricultural land were confiscated,
Czech farmers driven away and the land was
resettled with German farmers. All these forcible
displacements of population practically emptied
the countryside and overcrowded the towns where
war industries clamoured for labour to replace the
workers transported to Germany.

It was even more unfortunate that most of the
casualties and damage occurred during the last
months of the war and that the casualties were the
result of atrocities. In these few months the
Czech provinces alone lost 52 per cent of loco-
motives and 68.3 per cent of its rolling stock:
freight waggons suffered particularly bad damage
(74.5 per cent were destroyed). In addition
63.5 per cent of lorries and 47.9 per cent of buses
were ruined; 49 per cent of private cars
disappeared and industrial production sank to
50 per cent of its pre-war capacity. During the
last days of the war, during the uprising in Prague,
149 houses were destroyed and 633 of them were
heavily damaged: some 8,000 citizens died in the
fighting. The whole republic was subjected to
last minute atrocities usually committed by SS
troops. In April 1945, Plostina was burnt down
and twenty-eight inhabitants executed; in May 1945
Javoricko was burnt down and thirty-eight people
executed. Prerov, Rakovnik, Nynburk were
brutalised and thirty-four prisoners were executed
at Trest. Fifty Communist leaders who were rounded
up in Prague were executed on 2 May 1945. These
few examples are not exhaustive but show that apart
from bitterness and hatred the German armies were
leaving behind a leaderless population with its
economic and political systems either destroyed or
paralysed.[1]

This was the situation when President Benes
arrived in Prague from exile on 18 May 1945. He
had been following the advance of the Red Army,
taking over from it the liberated territories as
soon as the armies moved on. His intentions were
to re-establish the Czechoslovak republic and its

2

political and constitutional system in the form it had assumed in pre-Munich days. However, during the war he had time to reflect and now was determined to 'improve' the system to correspond to the new conditions resulting from the war and its destruction.

In 1938 Dr Benes was forced to abdicate as a result of the Munich agreement. But when during the war the Western allies declared the Munich agreement invalid, Benes considered himself once again the constitutional head of Czechoslovakia. Now in May 1945, he was back in Czechoslovakia as President and, in the absence of an elected parliament, a virtual dictator. Because of the circumstances, he had to rule the country by means of decrees. But he wanted to restore the old regime, albeit modified, as soon as practicable. The regime was going to be a presidential one, the President retaining most of the powers he had in the 1924 constitution. He was the titular head elected by parliament and responsible to it. However, he was also the Commander in Chief, had power of appointment over the executive, both the government and civil servants and in exceptional circumstances could act as dictator.[2]

East-West Compromise

The President was prepared to share power with a parliament freely elected and with a government responsible to the latter. Political parties would participate in ruling the country through these two institutions and their share of power would be determined by the election results. This basic political framework was to be operated by professional civil servants and adjudicated by an independent judiciary. Furthermore, President Benes envisaged several improvements: he was personally determined to become more of an arbiter than a chief executive, so far as the situation would allow him. He was also determined to modify the party system, for their multiplicity was a source of weakness in the first republic. The President therefore proposed one party for each classical grouping, the left, centre and right. However, before he succeeded in returning to Czechoslovakia, he was forced by the Czech Communists to change his intentions; their plan was for four parties to compete freely for power; the Communist Party and the Social Democratic Party on the left; the National Socialists (liberals) in the centre, and the People's Party (Catholic Party) on the right. In Slovakia the arrangement was even simpler: the Communist Party and the Democratic (liberal) Party were initially allowed to organise themselves. Two other parties were subsequently authorised but never really got off the ground, and in the 1946 election proved an insignificant factor. The last modification to President Benes's intentions seemed unimportant at the time but proved immensely important in 1948: political parties were to be grouped in a coalition called the National Front and no one could come to power, not even legally exist, except through this Front. These were all negotiated concessions and modifications to President Benes's schemes for post-war Czechoslovakia. However, developments on the spot brought further modifications.[3]

Although President Benes and his government had been recognised by all the Allies, including the USSR, it became clear (as in the case of Poland) that the President's and his government's real recognition would only come after Czechoslovakia's liberation. The problem was whether the USSR and the Red Army would allow President Benes and his group to move back into Czechoslovakia and establish themselves there in power. The Red Army began to liberate Slovak territory late in 1944, and henceforth Czechoslovak territory was taken over by and administered by the Red Army and their natural allies, Czechoslovak Communists. In July 1944, when the Slovaks rose against the Germans, President Benes saw this as a mixed blessing. He was overjoyed that the Slovaks had at long last acknowledged their past errors and guilt for the break-up of the Republic, but he also saw with

4

dismay that the new political authority, the Slovak National Council, began to act without consulting him, sometimes even acting against his doctrines. Thus the risen Slovaks proclaimed themselves an independent nation equal to the Czechs, and the two Slovak political parties then in existence, the Slovak Communist Party and the Slovak Democratic Party, began to put into practice certain Communist ideas which the President had rejected as impracticable during negotiations with the Czechoslovak Communist leaders in Moscow in December 1943. Thus the Slovak National Council and its representatives (commissioners) began to exercise powers of a national parliament and government and this was quite clearly contrary to President Benes's post-war projects. Moreover, they began to exercise administrative powers in areas of the uprising and liberated regions through ad hoc local and district councils (soviets) which the President opposed tooth and nail until December 1944, though he could do nothing about it. In addition the Slovaks put into practice another Communist idea, that of a political grouping or a sort of coalition called the National Front. This grouping, which would have far-reaching effect on the future political development of Czechoslovakia, determined local political arrangements allocating power more or less equally among the Slovak Communists, Democrats and non-party citizens.[4]

Even as President Benes and his entourage left London and arrived in Moscow in December 1944 in order to move into the liberated parts of the country, they could not be sure of their fate. First of all they had to come to another agreement with the Czechoslovak Communist leaders, and only then move on. Great uncertainties lay ahead as President Benes found out when he had sent his commissioners to the liberated Carpathian territory. At first the Red Army let the commissioners in, but then suddenly expelled them and abruptly annexed this formerly Czechoslovak region. Despite international recognition and agreements with the Communists the London group and Benes could be sure of nothing.[5]

National Committees (Soviets)

From the President's point of view the political
process of liberation became alarming.  As soon
as the Red Army liberated a commune, town or
city, it invariably dismissed the mayor, dissolved
the council and appointed a national committee in
their stead.  Between 1944 and August 1945 some
4,855 committees of this sort were appointed.
The chairman of these committees was usually a
local Communist, for the Red Army was aided in
their choice of mayors by liaison officers from
the Czechoslovak Army Corps organised in the USSR,
and they were invariably Communists.  In Slovakia
the representatives of the Slovak National Council,
who were sometimes consulted by the Red Army, also
tended to be Communist Party members and President
Benes had absolutely no control over this process.
On 4 December he had to put a brave face on it and
legalise these ad hoc bodies by declaring them
revolutionary local authorities.  He hoped that
their political composition would be modified in
the future after an election.

        Without consulting the President the Red
Army proceeded a step further.  Whenever it
liberated a district town it appointed the same
ad hoc committee at this administrative level.
In pre-war Czechoslovakia district administration
was professional and civil servants were appointed
by the Ministry of the Interior.  This apparently
was a step towards democratisation of Czechoslovak
administration:  the new distict chairman had the
same administrative powers as the old district
hetmans (roughly comparable to French sous-
prefets) and were 'elected' by these new committees.
The President was further disturbed to see that
appointments to these district committees were not
even based on pre-war election results.  Thus at
Michalovce, an Eastern Slovak district town, the
district committee consisted of five workers,
thirteen farmers, seven officials, three teachers,
one tradesman, seven administrators, one housewife
and three priests.  More significantly, of these
forty district councillors, seventeen were
Communists and twenty-three non-party members.

Thus in practice the agreement between Slovak Democrats and Communists on tripartite representation
had not been observed.  Though this sounded
alarming sometimes the explanation was simple:  in
the case of Michalovce the Red Army declared that
it could not appoint Slovak Democrats where there
were none.  It was a fact that non-Communist
parties were thoroughly disorganised and the
Communist Party was naturally taking advantage of
it, wherever it could.[6]

However, the Red Army could handle successfully even districts and cities where there were
no Communists.  Thus the Red Army liberated Brno,
the Moravian capital, on 26 April 1945.  The
pre-war majority party, the National Socialists,
headed an underground city council ready to take
over the administration of the city.  As soon as
the Wehrmacht left the city this council with an
armed retinue arrived at the town hall, but were
dissuaded from taking it over by the Red Army Major
Kovtun and Czechoslovak Army Lieutenant Harus, the
liaison officer and Communist leader.  Next day,
without any public announcement, an assembly
'elected' a thirty-member committee to run the city.
Of these twelve were Communists, six Social
Democrats, six National Socialists, four Christian
Democrats (who were not present) and two non-party
members.  V. Matula, who was elected chairman
(mayor), was a Communist as well as his administrative officer, the secretary, F. Pisek.  As a
concession for this unfavourable division of power
on the spot the National Socialists were permitted
to organise in Brno the Provincial Council
Moravian, administratively though not politically
comparable to the Slovak National Council.  Four
political parties delegated their representatives
to this council, whose chairman was elected
F. Loubal, member of the National Socialist Party.[7]

In Prague, the political situation was even
more confused than in Brno.  On 4 May 1945 Prague
citizens became restless and panicky, and the
following day they spontaneously rose against the
German garrison.  Only a few days before the
uprising the Gestapo arrested some fifty Communists

7

and executed them. Still on the day of the uprising, the vice-chairman of the National Czech
Council, which took over the leadership of the
revolt, was J. Smrkovsky, a Communist leader. He
entirely overshadowed the elder academic Prazak,
who was its chairman. In the bloody confusion
which followed, it seemed quite clear that no party
could take advantage. The German army command
happened to have near Prague the crack SS units
(SS Panzer Division Wiking, SS Panzer Kampfverband
Wallenstein and units of the Army Corps commanded
by General Reimann) and they instantly began to
pound the city with their guns. The risen citizens
erected some 16,000 barricades to oppose the
Wehrmacht, but were on the point of surrender when
the tanks of Generals Rybalko and Lelyushenko
reached Prague on 8 May 1945. Only then could the
Communist party take advantage of the situation and
Prague had its ad hoc city council and a Communist
mayor.[8]


Presidency

As President Benes finally arrived at the Hradcany
castle in Prague to rule Czechoslovakia, he was
heading a state whose power basis was unknown to
him and whose structures were established often
against his wishes and intentions. He was back in
power thanks to the victory of the Red and American
armies, but his power seems to have rested on the
unknown quality of "national committees" and army
units which returned almost entirely from the east,
the USSR. However precarious the basis power might
have seemed, the President still retained enough
power and privilege to be a decisive factor in the
determination of subsequent development in Czechoslovakia. Above all else he had his international
reputation and recognition and this made him
acceptable to the Czech and Slovak Communists.
Next he had retained great legislative and executive
powers and did not hesitate to use them. His
international prestige permitted him to solve the
age-long German problem; at Potsdam the victorious
powers recognised the justice of the Czechoslovak

8

claim against the Sudeten Germans and agreed to a
mass transfer to Germany. This particular success
made the President acceptable to every one except
a handful of collaborators with the Germans.[9]

As with the national committees the President
attempted to transform a spontaneous movement to
punish collaborators and Germans on the spot, which
invariably led to lynching or abuses, into something
resembling justice. His retribution decree defined
the crime of collaboration and set up tribunals to
deal with the accused. This did check the most
flagrant abuses and with time eliminated summary
justice. At the same time it made the President
strong enough to enable him to intervene in the
administration of justice, if he thought that the
spontaneous element was getting the upper hand.
Thus on the President's intervention a former
Minister of Justice, Dr Kalkus, who had served in
the Czech government during the war, was freed.[10]

Under pressure from the left and due to
chaotic conditions, President Benes also had to
make far-reaching decisions in the economy of
Czechoslovakia. A series of presidential decrees
nationalised all the mines, many industrial
enterprises, most of the food industry, all the
banks and insurance companies. On 19 May 1945 all
German-owned and collaborationist industrial
enterprises were confiscated by another
presidential decree; they were put under 'national
management'. By August 1945 some 9.045 factories
were administered under this arrangement which
meant roughly that they were nationalised. On
21 June 1945 President Benes issued a decree by
which confiscated land was given to Czech and Slovak
smallholders: this decree released some 3 million
hectares for chiefly landless agricultural
labourers. All these measures indicated that
presidential rule was vigorous and without any
challenge and as long as President Benes remained
in charge, Czechoslovakia would remain the
traditional democratic state engaged in social
experiments.[11]

In autumn 1945 President Benes was unanimously

re-elected President by the Provisional National
Assembly and in June 1946 by the newly-elected
parliament (The Constitutional National Assembly)
Unfortunately almost immediately after the latter
re-election the President's health broke down.[12]


Central Government

The government, which shared executive power with
the President, was appointed by Dr Benes at Kosice
in April 1945 and was a coalition.  Four Czech
and two Slovak political parties were represented
in it by their political leaders who managed to
survive the war abroad or who had risen in the
Slovak revolt.  It was a curious government,
politically very finely balanced and much dependent
on the President.  As a recognition of the fact
that the President and his government were coming
back to Czechoslovakia from the USSR, the
Czechoslovak Communist Party's share of power in
the government was quite out of proportion to its
pre-war strength.  Its leader, K. Gottwald, was
Deputy Prime Minister and the Communists also
controlled the important ministries of the Interior,
Education, Information and Agriculture.  In
addition the Slovak Communist leader, V. Siroky,
was also a Deputy Prime Minister and V. Clementis
State Secretary in the Ministry of Foreign Affairs.
Since the Prime Minister, Z. Fierlinger, was a left
Social Democrat, who would never hesitate to join
the Communists, the government seemed heavily tilted
to the left.  Still, it was obvious that in the
case of a conflict the Communists could paralyse
the government but could not hope to defeat their
coalition partners.  Two key ministries (Defence
and Foreign Affairs) were controlled by two
prestigious non-party men, General L. Svoboda and
Jan Masaryk, son of the first President of
Czechoslovakia.  In addition, several important
ministries were under non-Communist control: Finance
was controlled by a Slovak Democrat (I. Pietor),
Justice and Foreign Trade by National Socialists
(J. Stransky and H. Ripka).  It was clear that if
the non-Communists maintained unity, they could

easily outvote the Communists and left Social Democrats, for important policy decisions were made
by the government collectively by a majority vote.
However, even if the non-Communists split there was
another safeguard to prevent the Communists and
their allies from exploiting their predominance.[13]
This was a political government, while the
administration of policies was left to professional
civil servants who, on the whole, were above party
politics or on the contrary belonged to non-
Communist parties. The Communist Party made little
headway in the civil service: thus, for example,
in the Ministry of Foreign Affairs only 6 out of 68
top officials were Communist Party members; in the
Ministry of Education only 19 out of 105; in the
Ministry of Justice 3 out of 40 and in the Ministry
of Foreign Trade 4 out of 82. While the Minister
of the Interior, V. Nosek, was a Communist, General
Bartik, who was in charge of the state security
section, was replaced by Captain Pokorny, who was
a Communist, only in 1946. The Communist minister
had to form new branches and task forces (the
Special Battalion disbanded in 1946) to put his
political friends in charge of them (Border Guard
Battalion), and even then these untried forces could
not be relied upon. Furthermore, many security
officers who had remained on the staff of the
Ministry of the Interior were either non-Communists
or openly anti-Communists. It can be said that
this was a coalition government in which the
partners were condemned to govern together.[14]


Political Parties

The Communist Party of Czechoslovakia, the principal
partner of the coalition, before it could even
contemplate seizing power had to organise itself,
attract mass membership and win all the political
battles such as the parliamentary election in 1946.
From the beginning, the Communists devoted much
care and attention to building up party structures.
The leadership, which was notoriously divided in
pre-war days, sorted out problems at Kosice on
8 April 1945. At this early conference K. Gottwald

was confirmed as the leader, the Slovak leader,
K. Smidke, became vice leader and R. Slansky
remained Secretary General in charge of the
structures and administration.   Even after this
division of power within the party, unity was
still uncertain:   on the Czech side Gottwald had
his own men elected to the central committee
(Harus, Kopecky, Krosnar, Lastovicka, Nosek,
J. Prochazka, M. Svermova), while the Slovaks
remained unpredictable, with G. Husak and
L. Novomesky openly separatist.   To maintain unity
in Prague, Gottwald had to send Smidke, Husak and
Novomesky to important jobs in Slovakia:   Smidke
became Speaker of the Slovenska narodna rada
(Provincial Parliament) and Husak Prime Minister
(Predseda Sboru poverennikov).   V. Siroky became
the Slovak Communist Party chairman and J. Duris,
who became member of the Slovak preasidium, were
both Gottwald men and they removed to Prague to
represent Slovakia in the centre.   Thus leadership
uncertainties were solved and immediately the party
launched a massive membership drive.

    The Communist Party took full advantage of
the liberation by the Red Army to organise itself
on the spot.   In June 1945 when the war was over
and there was time for counting, the party could
claim some 597,500 members in the Czech and Slovak
provinces;   in Slovakia the party claimed 197,227
members.   No other party could advance comparable
claims, for the non-Communists never organised their
supporters in parties per se, but rather mobilised
them in times of elections.   However, enthusiasm
for joining the party began to wane soon afterwards
in Slovakia, although the party membership continued
to grow in the Czech provinces.   In August 1945
the Czech party had some 712,000 members;   early
in 1946 an additional 292,000 members were recruited
and in March 1946 at the party congress in Prague
some 1,038 delegates represented 1,081,544 members.
Of these 58 per cent were workers, 13 per cent
farmers and some 50,000 artisans and tradesmen had
joined the party as well.   The party published
six daily newspapers with an estimated circulation
of 700,000 and nineteen weeklies (circulation
150,000).   During the congress Gottwald proclaimed

his satisfaction with the performance of the party; it had mass membership well organised in territorial units and all it needed was success in the coming election.[15]

Of the other parties the best organised was the Slovak Democratic Party.  It took part in the Slovak uprising and acting throughout as the senior partner to Slovak Communists.  The Democratic Party held its congress even before the Communists in April 1945 and at Kosice its leaders obtained important ministries in the central government as well as in the Slovak autonomous parliament and government.  Although the Democratic Party was in the minority in local and district committees (narodni vybory), it nevertheless succeeded in recruiting the non-party majorities of these bodies and was full of confidence for the coming election.[16]

The three non-Communist Czech parties were all in bad shape.  The war dispersed their leaderships and completely destroyed their organisations and in 1945 they all had to start from scratch. The largest of them, the National Socialists, were by then a most peculiar amalgam of parties and social groups.  Historically they were originally the nationalist splinter group which divided itself from the Social Democratic Party in the late nineteenth century.  However, during the years of the first Republic (1918-1938) the party's membership changed.  The majority were no longer workers, but small businessmen, shopkeepers and professional people (civil servants, lawyers). Even before the war the party was disunited and had two wings, but the friction within redoubled after the war when the party tried to absorb outlawed parties, especially the National Democrats and Agrarians.  P. Zenkl, leader of the right wing, had only just returned from the Buchenwald concentration camp, and was endorsed as party leader in February 1947.  He had previously joined the government (1946) displacing the leader of the left wing elements, J. David.  Fortunately for the party, David became Speaker of the newly elected Constitutional Assembly; even the Communist

13

Party voted for him. The Secretary General of the party became V. Krajina, formerly a National Democrat, who distinguished himself during the war fighting the Germans in the underground movement. Krajina concentrated entirely on the administration and running of the party machine, which needless to say, was entirely different from that of the Communist Party.

Krajina's aim was a well-organised party with a massive representation in the Assembly and its leaders in top positions in the government. However, he never conceived the party as an instrument to the seizure of power, though the left wing was suspicious of his aims. The left wing was able to put an effective brake on Krajina's efforts. In a democratic system they conceived the party differently; its structure should be loose and the party should concentrate on the propagation of its policies and mobilisation of its followers (rather than members) for elections. A congress convoked to Prague on 28 February 1947 was to restore unity and reconcile opposing views. Some 3,000 delegates gathered at Prague-Vinohrady, a suburban stronghold of the party and in the enthusiastic euphoria of the congress seem to have achieved unity: the leaders of the right and left, Zenkl and David, kissed symbolically. However, the reality was different; the left wing retained control of all the important party committees and increased its representation by having Dr Slechta, who led the party after the Communist coup, elected to the preasidium. The right wing failed to make their presence and influence felt, although Zenkl became leader and Krajina remained as Secretary General. As it was, the National Socialist Party could compete for power alongside the other parties, but could not hope to become a counterpart of the Communist Party.[17]

The other Czech party, the People's Party, was in a similar position. It has never been an organised body but rather an association of voters with ideological (religious) links. Its leaders, Msgr Sramek and Rev. Hala were aging and ailing, and one could hardly speak of their leader-

14

ship. The party was also split: though it attracted to itself, as the only non-socialist party, a lot of support from the dissolved conservative parties, its rising leaders were often radicals, many of them prepared for political compromises with their ideological opponents, the Communists. Its strength lay in its appeal to cogent social groups (farmers, conservative professions and the middle class in general), who would always vote for it making it inevitably a strong party, but never the strongest nor capable of challenging the Communist party. It was a perfect coalition partner which would always come to a compromise agreement with the leading coalition partner whoever he may be.[18]

The last one of the Czech parties, the Social Democratic Party, like the Communist Party, had a compact following among the workers, and historically was the Socialist Party. It emerged from the war rather battered both in the leadership and organisation. The provisional leader, Z. Fierlinger, was so left that many of the right wing comrades suspected him of being a Communist Party member. The right wing itself was virulent but undistinguished and balanced out the left wing; the party did not disintegrate only thanks to its centrist group which took over the leadership after the congress at Brno in the autumn of 1947. A. Lausman routed Fierlinger in the struggle for leadership but in nothing else. Lausman's job as minister went to a left winger, while within the party machine the right wing Secretary General, B. Vilim, kept an eye on the centrists so that they did not take over the party. Thus, while the party was split at the top it was depleted at its base; the post-war wave of revolutionary enthusiasm caused many Social Democrats to join the Communist Party. Still in the post-war Czechoslovak system it was a decisive element; whichever way the party leant, there would be the majority.[19]


(Parliament) The Assembly

With all the political parties fully aware of their

15

strength and weakness the coalition arrangement
(and the National Front agreement) seems to have
suited everyone.  The non-Communist parties could
only seriously rival the Communist Party if they
united themselves internally and externally and
this was well nye impossible.  Thus they had to
acquiesce to the increase in Communist power.  In
August 1945, President Benes appointed a Provisional
National Assembly (a kind of parliament) in which
every party obtained forty seats.  This meant that
the Communist Party of Czechoslovakia control led
a majority in this assembly, for it obtained forty
seats for both Czech and Slovak branches as well
as the majority of the forty seats reserved for
social organisations (trade unions, veterans, youth
league, etc.).  This parliamentary strength was
quite out of proportion to its pre-war electoral
performance, but no one dared to raise his voice.
It was thought that this imbalance would be put
right after the parliamentary election scheduled
for May 1946.[20]

     The election, to be absolutely free, had to
take place after the withdrawal of the occupation
armies, the Red and American ones.  Curiously,
not external but domestic factors made this election
less absolutely free than customary.  While the
armies withdrew peacefully without interfering in
the election, the Czechs and Slovaks themselves
dissolved and banned many pre-war political parties,
among them the strongest one, the Agrarian Party.
Only four Czech and four Slovak parties approved
by the National Front were allowed to present their
candidates to the electorate which then could
choose to vote for them in a direct and secret
ballot.  It was expected that the voters of the
prohibited parties would swell the non-Communist
vote and the parties would win a resounding victory.
In a short but crisp campaign the National
Socialists and the People's Party had made use of
former Agrarian politicians to sway the electors
their way and convince them that they would
represent their interests, but this blandishment
worked in Slovakia only.  The Communist Party
appealed to the electors in a direct and most
effective way:  it declared itself responsible for

16

the confiscation of German industrial and land property which it distributed among the Czechs and Slovaks. It proposed further social reforms and experiments and to everyone's surprise emerged from the election as the largest political party of Czechoslovakia.

On 26 May 1946 the combined Czech and Slovak Communist Parties polled 2,695,293 votes, which meant the Communist Party of Czechoslovakia obtained 114 seats out of the 300 which the Constitutional Assembly consisted. This was a victory, but not a decisive one. The other parties did badly: the National Socialist Party polled only 1,298,980 (18.3 per cent) votes; the People's Party 1,111,009 (15.6 per cent); the Slovak Democratic Party 999,980 (14.1 per cent) and the Social Democrats 855,538 (12.1 per cent). Although in Slovakia the Communist Party polled only some 30.3 per cent and therefore became a minority party in that province, in the two Czech provinces, Bohemia and Moravia, the Communist Parties were disappointed and the Constitutional Assembly was as deadlocked as the Provisional one; despite hope the election solved nothing.[21]

The election results were also important for provincial and district councils (narodni vybory) which they legitimised. In these councils (local government) the Communist Party thus consolidated its position gained in the chaotic revolutionary post-war days. In the Czech provinces the Communist Party had an absolute majority in 37.5 per cent of local councils (mistni narodni vybory); it had overall control in 55.1 per cent local councils and 78 per cent district councils (okresni narodni vybory). This advance was only partially offset at the provincial level: though the Communist Party retained control of the Bohemian provincial council (zemsky narodni vybory) it lost this control in Moravia and Slovakia. Of the 163 district councils, the Communist Party controlled 128 which seemed a fair recompense for the loss of the two provinces, since the provinces were under the direct jurisdiction of the central government where they also controlled the key positions.[22]

Table 1.1

Election 1946

| Party | Votes Polled | Percentage |
|---|---|---|
| Czechoslovak Communist Party (KSC) | 2,695,293 | 38.7 |
| Czechoslovak Socialist Party (CSS) | 1,298,980 | 18.3 |
| Czechoslovak Christian Party (CSL) | 1,111,009 | 15.6 |
| Czechoslovak Social Democratic Party (CSD) | 855,538 | 12.1 |
| Slovak Democratic Party (SDP) | 999,557 | 14.1 |
| Slovak Freedom Party (SSS) | 60,200 | 3.7 |
| Slovak Social Democratic Party (SSD) | 56,000 | 3.1 |

Parliament 1946-48

| Party | Number of Seats |
|---|---|
| Czechoslovak Communist Party (KSC) | 114 |
| Czechoslovak Socialist Party (CSS) | 55 |
| Czechoslovak Christian Party (CSL) | 46 |
| Czechoslovak Social Democratic Party (CSD) | 37 |
| Slovak Democratic Party (SDP) | 43 |
| Slovak Freedom Party (SSS) | 3 |
| Slovak Social Democratic Party (SSD) | 2 |

Constitutional Assembly : 300

18

It soon became clear that the same state of power stalemate would continue as before the election; a decisive point in the struggle for supremacy had not been reached and once again the coalition partners, the Communists and non-Communists, were condenmed to peaceful coexistence. However, the Communist Party seems to have been more encouraged by the relative electoral victory than the other parties. During a central committee meeting on 22-23 January 1947, Gottwald proclaimed publicly his party's aim to win the scheduled election in 1948 decisively (51 per cent) and govern the country alone. The other parties refused to pay attention to such pronouncements, though retrospectively it was claimed that as early as January 1947 the Communist Party decided to stage a coup d'état to obtain absolute power in Czechoslovakia. It seems more probable that this was a tactical move to test the nerve and determination of the non-Communist proclamation: the congress of the National Socialist Party confirmed its anti-Communist line. Shortly afterwards, at the Social Democratic Party congress the left wing was decisively beaten, the party set out to divest itself of Communist influence and began to co-operate openly with non-Communist parties. If this type of unity of action continued, the Communists could not hope to win the coming election.[23]

Anti-Communist mood began to manifest itself in other spheres of life: various courts began to annul confiscation decrees on industrial enterprises issued by Communist-dominated local or district authorities. The courts ordered these enterprises to be denationalised and handed over to their rightful owners. While the Communists successfully resisted the actual hand over by means of strikes and demonstrations, they could not prevent legal proceedings from continuing and ultimately the Czech and Slovak owners would have reclaimed their confiscated property had it not been for the coup d'état in 1948.[24] Communist offensive in agriculture was also skilfully fought by the non-Communists: the Communist party wanted to confiscate and distribute all the land of estates over fifty hectares. On 1 July 1947 the Constitutional Assembly passed a bill (Land Reform Act) which did not contain Communist demands.[25]

However, there were also victories by the Communist Party. Thus the struggle for the so-called millioners tax to finance subsidies for farmers' crops damaged by the drought in the summer of 1947 was won by the Communist Party. When the party proposed that all citizens with property in excess of one million crowns should pay a tax levy to the agricultural relief fund, the non-Communist majority in the government blocked the proposal (9 September 1947). The Communist Party then proceeded to organise protest campaigns and succeeded in seriously splitting the rank and file of the other parties on this issue. On 10 September 1947, under pressure, the government reversed its decision, the tax was enacted and some 4,000 million crowns in compensation were paid out to the farmers.[26]

Perhaps even more ominous, the struggle between the Communists and non-Communists came into the open in the international sphere. In June 1947 the Czechoslovak government was invited to join a European conference which was to decide on the allocation of American economic aid (Marshall Plan). The government at first accepted the invitation, but after a visit to Moscow, Premier Gottwald declined to attend the conference. Gottwald explained to his colleagues in government that the USSR would furnish Czechoslovakia with aid itself. As a consequence of the drought, Czechoslovakia asked immediately for grain and fodder, and the USSR promptly agreed to send relief.[27]

Another external political event helped to harden the political situation in Czechoslovakia. After a series of violent strikes, the Communist Party of France was excluded from a government coalition against which the strikes were directed. Czechoslovak Communists took the French events as a recipe for other European countries especially after the National Socialist leader, P. Zenkl,

visited France and had talks with French socialist
leaders. The visit was purely coincidental and
similar tactics could not be employed in
Czechoslovakia.[28]  On the other hand, in
September 1947, Czechoslovak Communists attended
a Cominform consultation in Poland and it is
equally unlikely that the coup d'état in
Czechoslovakia was discussed.  However, all these
international factors complicated internal politics
in Czechoslovakia, and it became increasingly
obvious that the intensified struggle for
supremacy would be resolved by something other
than the election in May 1948.

Then in September 1947 the Communist Party
made a tremendous political effort in Slovakia to
tilt the uneasy balance of power its own way.
On 14 September 1947 the Slovak Ministry of the
Interior, controlled by the provincial premier,
G. Husak, announced that it had discovered a plot
against Czechoslovakia, in which Slovak Democratic
leaders were implicated.  Two secretaries of the
Slovak Democratic Party, Kempny and Bugar, were
arrested and leaders implicated in the affairs had
to resign (Deputy Premier in the central government,
J. Ursiny).  On 11 October 1947 the preasidium
of the Slovak Communist Party met and decided to
exploit the 'plot' politically and force the Slovak
Democratic provincial ministers to resign.  On
30 October 1947 they organised hastily a congress
of factory councils which called for Democratic
Party resignations.  On the following day the
whole Slovak provincial government resigned and
the National Front coalition asked the old Premier,
G. Husak, to reconstruct the government.  While
Husak was considering a reshuffle Slovak trade
unions staged an hour strike to help him in his
considerations.  On 14 November peasant commission
congress also urged Husak to purge the government
of treacherous elements.  It is true that counter-
demonstrations were organised by the Democratic
Party at Bratislava, Kosice and Zvolen, but they
failed to impress public opinion.  On 18 November
1947 Husak announced the composition of the new
provincial government which was most promptly
approved by the central government:  out of the

fifteen ministers, members of the majority Democratic Party, Husak retained only five. The purge was constitutional, successful and the Communist Party turned its electoral defeat in 1946 into a great victory.[29]

The smoothness of this coup de force must have influenced the Czechoslovak Communist leadership in Prague. If a suitable pretext could be found and political circumstances were equally favourable tactics employed in the Slovak coup could be used in Czechoslovakia as a whole; political opponents intimidated by strikes, demonstrations and public meetings could be removed from power and a political crisis could be resolved in a similar constitutional manner without disturbing the international public opinion. Communist decisions were probably made at this stage.

On 28 November 1947 during another central committee meeting Premier Gottwald declared rather superfluously that the Communist Party would not be kicked out of power. The declaration was not taken at all seriously, because every one in Czechoslovakia, even the bitterest opponent of the Communists, knew full well that the Communist Party could not be eliminated from power without a bloody civil war. However, by then it became equally apparent that the Communist Party would not win the 51 per cent of votes in the coming election; opinion polls in fact indicated that the party would lose support. At this stage Gottwald was simply issuing a warning: his party was prepared for any crisis.[30]

Since the other parties became confident that they would win the coming election they prepared for nothing. If they had any tactics they ran along the lines of a constitutional crisis: after the Communist defeat in the government or parliament the deadlock would be resolved in the election. This tactic was never fully worked out and there existed no concensus for common action among the non-Communist parties. At the same time the pressure from the Communist

Party forced the non-Communists to seize the initiative.[31]    On 10 February 1948 the Social Democratic minister, V. Majer, presented a proposal at the government meeting by which the higher grades of the civil service should get substantial salary increases.  The Communist Minister of Finance, J. Dolansky, rejected this proposal, but the government, which always approved policies and financial measures collectively by a majority vote, over-ruled Dolansky.  Constitutionally the minister had to implement a measure which he and  presumably the Communist Party did not approve.  This important government meeting at which the Communist Party was defeated, was attended by A. Zapotocky, chairman of the Trade Union Council (Ustredni rada odboru) and member of the Communist Party preasidium.  Most significantly he also disagreed with the salary increases and decided on extra-government and parliamentary means to block the proposal.  He persuaded the TUC to convoke to Prague a congress of all the workers councils and trade unions on 22 February 1948.[32]

        This protest gesture, although it came so shortly after the events in Slovakia, did not appear particularly ominous since it seemed inconceivable that a coup would be used on such a minor issue.  The pretext would have to be more plausible while the salary issue was used to divide the opponents:  several non-Communist trade union leaders (National Social Krejci and Social Democrat Cipro) as well as rank and file members opposed the government decision.

        Still the non-Communists, encouraged by this show of unity and victory in the government, decided to press on their advantage and embarrass Communist ministers and Premier Gottwald even more.  The National Socialist deputy, Hora, member of the security committee of the Constitutional Assembly, learned about a transfer of eight police officers from the force to other duties.  It appeared to be a routine move, but Hora decided otherwise.  He informed his party ministers, Drtina and Ripka, about this ominous

23

measure, for all the officers were members of the National Socialist Party. The ministers decided to raise the matter at the next meeting of the government, called for 13 February. The scheduled government meeting was to discuss the social security bill, but on the insistence of the non-Communist ministers police matters were put on the agenda, although the Minister of the Interior, V. Nosek, was indisposed and would not be present. After a prolonged and heated discussion, the non-Communist ministers scored another voting victory by which Nosek was instructed to put the police matters right and cancel the transfers. It was this 'victory' that was taken up by the Communist Party as a declaration of war which was chosen by both sides as a pretext for a final showdown.

The Communist Party had already mobilised their supporters in the trade unions for the congress; now it decided to mobilise supporters among the farmers and convoked their congress to Prague to take place shortly after the trade unions congress. The party itself was in a state of readiness since November 1947. The non-Communists only just started their preparations for the confrontation: consultations finally took place among them, though no common action was agreed upon. On 16 February 1948 National Socialist leaders met and probably made the surprising decision to resign from the government, if minister Nosek refused to implement the government decision on police transfers. The following day National Socialist leaders met the Peoples Party leadership as well as the right wing Social Democrats and agreed to insist on the implementation of the police decision at whatever cost. The cost they had in mind was a constitutional crisis.

The Communist Party preasidium treated this development more seriously than its opponents and refused to think and act in limited terms of a constitutional crisis. Instead it called on its supporters to be vigilant, organise protest meetings and thus force the non-Communists to

24

give up their obstruction of government business: no resignations were contemplated by the Communists. On 19 February 1948 numerous meetings took place all over the country and protest telegrams from them were sent to every political leader, the President included.

Another government meeting was scheduled for 20 February 1948 which was to be attended by the Minister of the Interior. National Socialist, People's Party and the Slovak Democratic ministers foregathered in the office of the Deputy Premier, P. Zenkl, who telephoned Gottwald enquiring whether the police measures had been implemented. On being told no, they all decided to boycott the meeting, and later that day they submitted their resignations from the government to the President. This was as far as they were prepared to go; henceforth power initiative passed on to the Communists.

The following day Premier Gottwald organised a huge meeting in the centre of Prague at which he analysed the political crisis: the counter-revolutionary reaction had tried to overthrow the people's democratic regime. They failed, but as a result they would be ejected not only from the government but from power altogether. Gottwald then asked his followers to form purge committees (akcni vybory) all over the country and purge all the local reactionaries as well. Husak, the Slovak Premier, immediately asked the Democratic Party ministers to resign in Slovakia. With a nationwide purge set in motion, it was only the President who still held up the resolution of the crisis along Gottwald's line. However, the President was also under strong, continuous pressure to give in, accept the resignations of the non-Communist ministers and allow Gottwald to reshuffle the government. On 22 February the trade unions congress exerted its pressure on the ailing President: apart from passing resolutions calling for more nationali-sation, land reform and modified civil service salary increases, it announced an hour token general strike in support of Premier Gottwald.[33]

On 23 February political chaos became
evident although the President continued to hold
out.  In Slovakia Husak's new purged government
contained no official leaders of the Democratic
Party and was absolutely dominated by the
Communists.  Purges at all levels were in full
swing, although the central purge organisation
(ustredni akcni vybor narodni fronty) was only
just formed.  Next day the general strike was
followed completely and for an hour life the the
country came to a standstill.  In Prague the
Communist Party staged continuous meetings in
the streets and in Wenceslas Square.  This was
obviously the climax of the crisis and, if the
non-Communists were not to acknowledge defeat
and retire peacefully, they had to reply in
kind.34

But they were all unprepared and surprised
by the turn of events.  This was not a
confrontation in constitutional terms and they
were at a loss as to what to do next.  The
National Socialist leaders were not even in
Prague;  Zenkl and Ripka left for the provinces
to address party meetings.  The People's Party
cracked up first;  its ailing leader, Msgr.
Sramek, failed to control its left wing which
agreed to join the next coalition government and
the party leadership disintegrated even before
the final solution of the crisis.  Next Slovak
Democrats panicked and their left wing took over
the party, which they renamed as the Slovak
Renaissance Party.  Paradoxically, the Social
Democrats were not told of the resignations,
although its ministers strongly supported the
non-Communists on the police matters.  The
party as a whole decided not to resign from the
government, thus making Gottwald's survival
constitutional.

Only on 25 February 1948 a flicker of hope
came when non-Communist students in Prague
marched to the Hradcany palace in support of the
President.  This was the only demonstration in
support of the non-Communists;  it was relatively
small, came too late and was easily dispersed by

the police without much bloodshed.[35]    With the
mass meeting continuing in Wenceslas Square,
Gottwald, Nosek and A. Zapotocky arrived at the
Hradcany castle to see the President and present
him with the list of ministers of the reconstructed
government.   After an hour's negotiation, with
the roar of the Communist demonstration in
Wenceslas Square clearly audible, the President
yielded, accepted the resignations and appointed
the new government.   Although the new government
had to be approved by the Constitutional
Assembly, the President's appointment really
ended the crisis and put a constitutional seal on
the coup.   For in the meantime, by means of their
purge committees, the Communists were able to
take over the state administration, local government, universities, social organisations and the
non-Communist parties themselves.   The army
remained neutral, the police was hardly used at
all, the takeover was political.   Only organised
street demonstrations and purges destroyed the
Czechoslovak political system demonstrating its
vital flaw:   the non-Communist majority could
mobilise its supporters for electoral purposes
only, not for the defence of the system.

      The newly-confirmed Prime Minister,
K. Gottwald, went directly from the royal castle,
the seat of the President, to Wenceslas Square
and announced his final fictory to the crowd
which went hysterical with joy.   On that very
day, non-Communist leaders rapidly dispersed,
escaping abroad into exile and leaving the
Communists and their allies to complete the power
takeover peacefully.   The Constitutional Assembly
thoroughly intimidated, approved the new
government overwhelmingly (230 votes out of
300) and calm returned to Czechoslovakia after
the excitement of the crisis.   Public order was
never disturbed and not even the United Nations
could demonstrate that a violent revolution with
Soviet help took place in Czechoslovakia.    In
any case, the real revolutionary upheaval came
about a year later.

1. R. Luza, The Transfer of the Sudeten Germans, London, 1964, pp. 257ff.

2. Prehled ceskoslovenskych dejin, Vol. 3, Prague, 1960, pp. 516-59; M. Klimes, M. Zachoval, Prispevek k problematice unorovych udalosti v Ceskoslovensku v unoru 1948, Ceskoslovensky casopis historicky VI/2, 1958, p. 191.

3. J. Kral, Otazky hospodarskycho a socialniho vyvoje v ceskych zemich, Prague, 1957, Vol. 1, pp. 24ff; Vol. 3, pp. 245-331.

4. Public Record Office, London (hereafter PRO) FO 371, 56085: Czechoslovakia: Annual Political Review for 1945.

5. Chronologicky prehled dulezitych dekretu prezidenta republiky z roku 1945, CTK Bulletin, Prague, 1975, pp. 9-14.

6. J. Kalvoda, Czechoslovakia's Roles in Soviet Strategy, Washington, D.C., 1978, pp. 147-74.

7. K. Bertelmann, Vznik narodnich vyborn, Otazky narodni a demokraticke revoluce v CSR, Prague, 1955, pp. 113-138; S. Matousek, Slovenske narodne organzy, Bratislava, 1960, pp. 83ff.

8. PRO WO 193/303 World Strategy Review, May 1945; O. Janecek, Zrod politiky narodni fronty a Moskevske vedeni KSC, Revue dejin socialismu, Prague 1968/VIII, pp. 803-48. Also cf. F. Nemec, V. Moudry, The Soviet Seizure of Subcarpathian Ruthenia, Toronto, 1955.

9. J. Vesely, Kronika unorovych dnu 1948, Prague, 1959, p. 18; also Bertelmann, op. cit., p. 113ff.

10. V. Pesa, Ustaveni a cinnost Narodniho vyboru v Brne v dubnu az kvetnu 1945, Brno v minulosti a dnes, Brno 1960, pp. 24-44.

11. Odboj a revoluce, 1938-1945, Prague, 1965; K. Bartosek, Prazske povstani 1945, Prague, 1965, pp. 233ff; Prehled ceskoslovenskych dejin, Vol. 3, pp. 574ff.

12. PRO FO 371, No. 47124 Czech Intelligence Summary, 17 January 1945.

13. FO 371 No. 56085, Annual Political Review for 1945; J. Opat, O novou demokracii, Prague, 1966, pp. 115-9. J. Smutny, Unorovy prevat 1948, London, 1957, Vol. 5.

14. Opat, op. cit., pp. 34ff; also PRO FO 371, No. 56085 op. cit.: the Foreign Office comments that the Communists secured all key positions.

15. J. Hendrych, A. Sramek, Ceskoslovenska statni sprava, Prague, 1973, pp. 40ff; Klimes, Zachoval, op. cit., pp. 215-6.

16. Dejiny KSC, Prague, 1961, pp. 479ff.

17. V. Pavlicek, Nektere poznamky k cinnosti Narodni Fronty z hlediska systemu vice politickych stran po unoru 1948, Prispevky k dejinam KSC, Prague, 1963/V, pp. 676-9.

18. L. Kapitola, B. Kucera, Uloha narodne-socialisticke strany v obdobi 1945-1948, Otazky . . ., op. cit., pp. 238-59.

19. B. Bunza, Le parti populaire tchecoslovaque, Rome, 1971, pp. 19-25.

20. Pavlicek, op. cit., p. 677; cf. also J. Horak's dissertation submitted at Columbia University, New York in 1960, The Czechoslovak Social Democratic Party 1938-1945; the Foreign Office thought that the President of the party, Z. Fierlinger, was a Soviet secret agent under the direct orders of P. Beria (PRO FO 181-933 Foreign Office to Moscow Embassy, 25 May 1945).

21. PRO FO 371 No. 56081 Annual Political Review for 1946.

22. M. Caha, M. Reiman, O nekterych otazkach vedouci ulohy strany v obdobi budovani socialismu v Ceskoslovensku, Prispevky k dejinam KSC, Prague, 1962/6, pp. 845-76.

23. R. N. Fouska, Narodni ocista v letech 1945-1946, Otazky . . ., op. cit., pp. 223-37.

24. K. Kaplan, Uloha hnuti rolnickych mas v procesu prerustani narodni a demokraticke revoluce v socialistickou, Prispevky k dejinam KSC, 1963/4, pp. 483-507.

25. J. Belda, Mocensko-politicke zmeny v CSR po unoru 1948 Revue dejin socialismu, Prague, 1968/8, pp. 227-50; Belda considers this espionage affair as one of the chief steps towards provoking a national crisis which the Communist Party would use to carry out a coup d'état.

26. J. Belda, op. cit., p. 247; J. Belda, M. Boucek, Z. Deyl, M. Klimes, K otazce ucasti CSR na Marshallove planu, Revue dejin socialismu, 1968/8, pp. 81-100.

27. Unor 1948. Sbornik dokumentu, Prague, 1958, p. 183.

28. Belda, op. cit., p. 229, thought that the Slovak affair and its successful resolution from the Communist point of view influenced decisively Gottwald, who shortly afterwards made a successful attempt at a national coup d'état. The British also thought the non-Communist defeat in Slovakia as crucial for the whole country (PRO FO 817 - 46 Slovak Affair). B. Jarosova, Odbory a revolucni vyvoj na Slovensku v rokoch 1945-47, Prispevky k dejinam KSC, 1962/4, pp. 508-30; Emil Karaba, Predzvest Unora, Rudé Pravo, 14 September 1971 which reflects Husak's version of this affair.

29.  Cf. belated publication of the opinion poll which showed that the Communist Party would get less than 50 per cent of the votes in the forthcoming general election (Dejiny a soucastnost, Prague, 1968/7, p. 44).

30.  Belda, op. cit., p. 228, affirms categorically that the Communist Party was using the security services to provoke the crisis: the services were put under Gottwald's direct orders bypassing the Minister of the Interior, Vaclav Nosek.

31.  The basic version of the February coup can be found in, for example, J. Besely, Krnonika unorovych dnu 1948, Prague, 1959; M. Boucek, M. Klimes, Dramaticke dny unora 1948, Prague, 1973; non-Communist versions are in J. Korbel, The Communist Subversion in Czechoslovakia, London, 1959; P. E. Zinner, Communist Strategy and Tactics in Czechoslovakia, London, 1963.

32.  M. Boucke, "On the Rise of the Czechoslovak People's Militia in February 1948", Historica, Prague, 1964/9, pp. 305-31.

33.  J. Mlynsky, Uloha akcnich vyboru Narodni fronty pri zajistovani unoroveho vitezstvi, Sbornik historicky, Prague, 1964/12, pp. 149-66.

34.  J. Manak, Socialni aspekty politiky KSC vuci inteligenci v letech 1947-53, Revue dejin socialismu, Prague, 1969/1, pp. 675-706.

35.  R. Bejkovsky, Boj KSC o lidovou armadu 1945-48, Prispevky k dejinam KSC, Prague, 1963/2, pp. 274-9; K. Kaplan, "On the Role of Dr E. Benes in February 1948", Historica, Prague, 1963/5, pp. 239-65.

# CHAPTER II

## The Dissolution of Czechoslovakia and
## The Rise of the Communist Party

Premier Gottwald set into motion a nation-wide
purge even before he had obtained the
constitutional sanction from President Benes to
re-constitute his government and eliminate from
power the twelve ministers who had revolted against
him.  Still, it was not quite clear what he meant
when, on 21 February, he issued his call for the
formation of 'action committees' to purge all the
"reactionaries and traitors".  Two days later the
Central Action Committee met and began to organise
the purge.  This central purge 'tribunal' was
presided over by the trade union leader,
A. Zapotocky;  its executive secretary was
Gottwald's son-in-law, A. Cepicka.  It consisted
of ninety-three members who were overwhelmingly
Communist;  non-Communist parties were also
represented on it, though only by individual
members, not as corporate bodies.  On 5 March
fifteen representatives of the Slovak Action
Committee of the National Front were added to
this central organisation thus recognising its
jurisdiction in that province.  While this central
body supervised the purge in the centre - it
purged the Constitutional Assembly, central
government and leaderships of political parties -
action committees were formed at all levels, in
the provinces and districts as well as locally
in factories, industrial enterprises, universities
and schools, newspaper offices and printing works,
theatres and social organisations.[1]

It was not difficult to purge 'reactionaries' in factories and industrial enterprises,
where there were few in any case.  In such
places the Communist Party turned the purge into
a membership drive;  it dissolved the branches of
the other parties and invited them to join the
party.  At Zlin (Gottwaldov) in the Bata shoe

enterprise the party's membership jumped from 9.658
to 11,407; at Pilsen the Skoda works branch
increased its membership from 9.771 to 11,220;
at Jinonice the Walter Works branch from 1,070 to
1,334.[2]

Curiously, the central administration did
not present many problems either, though it
contained most of the 'reactionaries' Premier
Gottwald referred to. Politically the government
submitted to the purge almost nonchalantly. The
ministers, who had resigned, left their departments
peacefully even before the final solution of the
crisis under pressure from the purge (action)
committees which were formed in every ministry,
usually from ancillary personnel (porters, cleaning
staff, etc.). One minister (V. Majer) refused to
leave his office and was physically ejected from
it presumably by the purge committee. With the
ministers went some 28,000 civil servants who were
dismissed by the purge committees and were allowed
to join the labour force in industry.[3]

The extent of the purge in public administration can be best gauged from the figures of
Communist Party membership in the various
ministries. Thus in the Ministry of Agriculture,
which throughout 1945-48 had a Communist minister,
J. Duris, only some 11 per cent of civil servants
were members of the Communist Party. By 1948,
after the shock of the coup, 29 per cent were
Communist Party members. However, in 1949 79 per
cent of civil servants in this ministry were party
members, which means that some 50 per cent of civil
servants were dismissed in 1948 and the rest of the
non-Communist officials in the 1950s. The Ministry
f Industry dismissed 352 of its civil servants
between February and March 1948 while the Ministry
of Post only 219. By September 1948 central
ministries dismissed some 4,525 civil servants and
pensioned off 1,014 others. In Slovakia the purge
on this level was less violent and only some 159
civil servants were dismissed, 47 pensioned off
and 301 suspended. However, from the scale of
dismissals it is clear that central administration

became ineffective; this must have been the
Communist objective, before the party could re-
organise public administration and staff it with
its own personnel.[4]

Although the army played no active role in
the coup d'état, the purge hit it in a devastating
way. Immediately after the coup, 2,965 higher
ranks (27.5 per cent) were discharged and the purge
continued until 1950 by which time 60 per cent of
the officers corps was replaced by men handpicked
by the Communist Party. The party established
nine special officers schools for factory workers
and during 1948-49 these schools turned out 1,800
new officers. When in 1950 the army was reorganised and re-equipped even its post-war leader,
and Minister of Defence, General L. Svoboda, was
dismissed and his place was taken by Gottwald's
son-in-law, A. Cepicka. In the tiny security
service the purge was very smooth: the few non-
Communist officers either escaped from the country
or were discreetly liquidated. Only in 1968 did
these murders come to light and the victims were
rehabilitated and their executioners brought to
trial. However, the Communist replacements did
not survive their victims long, and were purged in
turn in 1950. Most of them were killed and on
Soviet advice a Ministry of Security was [5]
established and the service entirely rebuilt.

The purge affected equally severely local
government, although most of it was under Communist
control. On 25 February 1948 the Minister of
the Interior, V. Nosek, issued an instruction by
which dismissals and purges could be effected in
the elected local government bodies. In the first
month of the purge some 25,000 local government
personnel were dismissed. In July 1948, when
appeals were allowed, some 15,000 did appeal, but
only 500 appeals were upheld. The full extent of
this purge is not known even today, but it seems
evident that the local government councils most
hit by the purge were those which were not under
Communist control. In some cases entire councils
had to be dissolved and replaced by lonely Communist
individuals. But on the whole, Communist

councillors contented themselves with assuming the chairmanships of the councils; public order departments were also consistently purged and taken over. Next worst affected were those local government officials, who after the war administered the councils (narodni vybory) masquerading as secretaries or elected members. Since their jobs were now taken over by "unqualified" local politicians it is probably only a slight exaggeration to say that effective local government ceased: on 1 January 1949 this heavily mauled administration was 'completely re-organised', when the administrative 'land' system was replaced by the regional system which divided Czechoslovakia into twenty regions, 160 districts and some 40,000 communes.[6]

The destruction of the parliamentary system was also comparatively easily achieved. The Constitutional Assembly was so shocked and intimidated by the events of the coup d'état that it voted overwhelmingly for the new governent, ipso facto destroying itself. Only seventy members out of three hundred failed to arrive and take part in this vital vote of confidence; among the 230 positive votes the non-Communists still had a majority; they voted for the government although its programme meant the dissolution of the existing political system. In May 1948 the parliamentary system was destroyed formally. The general election conducted under a different electoral law transformed the National Assembly from a parliament, in which political parties competed with each other, into a chamber which had within no competition and no parties, but a collective political body called the National Front. This National Front had existed before the coup, but then it was a loose coalition, a sort of meeting place; now it became the central election organ which approved and put forward lists of candidates; it also formulated 'common' policies, though only for a short time. In the election in May 1948 the National Front put forward a united list of candidates in which the Communist Party reserved for itself an overwhelming majority: 215 seats went to the Czechoslovak Communist Party.

The three Czech parties were given an arbitrary
representation of twenty-three seats each, while
the two Slovak parties obtained twelve and four
seats respectively.

With the National Assembly dominated
absolutely by the Communist Party its formal
transformation appeared in the new Constitution
which was also promulgated in May 1948. It was
described as a *purely* legislative body, many of
its powers transferred to its preasidium; in fact
its functions resembled strikingly the Supreme
Soviet, although structurally it was still
different from that body. However, in 1949, a
new procedural law was passed by the National
Assembly which was a self-administered coup de
grâce: it limited the powers of the members,
committees and plenary sessions and began to meet
twice a year approving unanimously and
retrospectively all the legislation and decrees
promulgated by its preasidium. Thus this most
traditional Czechoslovak political institution
was completely transformed, if not destroyed, and
became a copy of its Soviet counterpart.⁷

Possibly the most severe blow was dealt to
the judiciary, which the Communists considered
the most 'reactionary profession of the defeated
bourgeoisie'. The Ministry of Justice was under
non-Communist control since 1945 and the
Communists had hardly any members among the
civil servants and judges. The minister,
P. Drtina, purged himself, after he had
unsuccessfully tried to commit suicide; an
action committee then purged the ministry. The
administration of justice was immediately
simplified. The constitutional court together
with the supreme administrative court were
abolished. The former verified the validity
of elections; the latter judged cases arising
from conflicts between citizens and administration.
Both courts lost their raison d'être: henceforth
there could be no doubt about election results;
it was reasoned that the working class could not
be in conflict with itself, since it became
responsible for administration. A great majority

of professional judges were dismissed and replaced
by handpicked workers.  The Communist dean of law
faculty at Prague University, J. Bartuska,
admitted some 1,200 workers to special courses
which in eighteen months made out of them
qualified judges with academic titles.  They
began to practise their profession even before
they had taken their degrees.  The way was open
to the maladministration of justice as well as to
judicial murders later described as the "excesses
of the cult of personality".[8]

It is a little surprising to observe the
extent of demoralisation of non-Communists
consequent on the coup.  It enabled the Communist
Party to take over even such institutions where
it was hardly represented.  Thus at Brno
University, Professor F. Travnicek, a philologist
and the only prominent Communist on the staff,
responded to the Central Action Committee's appeal
on 25 February 1948, and declared himself chairman
of the University Purge Committee.  On his
initiative the few Communist Party members in
the four faculties formed their staff purge
committees, but in the law faculty Travnicek had
to appoint his own committee consisting of porters
and students only.  The committees then purged
the four elected leaders of the Students Unions,
and expelled eighty-eight other students from the
University;  only eighteen members of staff were
dismissed.  This mild shock tactic achieved its
purpose:  the university was sufficiently
intimidated, it continued its work without
interruption and as a result of the shock the
Communist Party increased its membership sixfold.
In the autumn of 1948 the party could carry out
a real purge:  the law faculty expelled 45.5 per
cent of its undergraduates, arts faculty 28.5
per cent, natural sciences 27.4 per cent, medical
faculty 20.9 per cent and the institute of
education 5 per cent.  In 1950 the recalcitrant
law faculty was dissolved, its students dispersed
and the staff joined the Slavonic Institute.[9]  In
exactly the same mild and almost casual way were
purged the trade unions, Veteran Association
(membership 153,506), Peasant Commissions, Womens

Councils, Youth Organisations and the Sokol
Gymnast Association (membership 569,213) which
despite 11,446 expulsions continued its defiance
of the CP until absorbed by the Workers
Gymnastic Association.10

Necessarily special attention had to be
paid to the purge of the non-Communist leadership and of the political parties themselves.
At the top purges were conducted by the new
leaders (ministers) whom Gottwald selected for
his reconstituted government. The mildest
purge initially took place in the Social
Democratic Party, where the chairman, B. Lausman,
remained in office; only four members of the
preasidium were expelled, and the Secretary
General suspended, because of ill health,
However, at regional and district levels Social
Democrats were purged by the action committees
of the National Front and the purge was more
severe. On 11 March 1948 Lausman was dismissed
and replaced by Z. Fierlinger, and in May 1948
regional and district committees decided to join
equivalent Communist organisations. On 27 June
1948 the Social Democratic Party fused formally
with the Communist Party: four Social Democrats
(Fierlinger, Jankovcova, John, Erban E.) were
added to the Communist Party preasidium and eleven
others were co-opted in the central committee.

The other non-Communist parties suffered
complete destruction. The National Socialist
Party's preasidium contained only one dissident,
A. Slechta, who was, nevertheless, able to take
over the party as a whole after the other leaders
had fled the country. It appears that regional
and district leaders also abandoned the party (and
possibly also the country), and the party
dissolved itself. It changed its name to the
Czech Socialist Party; some members joined the
Communist Party, other simply left politics
altogether: its membership slumped from 593,982
to some 20,000. In 1950 there were only 0.3 per
cent of Czech Socialists active in public life.

In the People's Party the destruction was

more gradual, although its preasidium disintegrated
even before the purge. Its majority dispersed to
avoid arrest: the party chairman, Msgr. Sramek,
was caught by the security police trying to escape
from the country together with the Secretary
General, Fr. Hala. They were both arrested and
kept interned in a monastery, where they both later
died. The leaders of the left wing, A. Petr and
Fr. Plojhar, assumed the leadership of the party
after they had joined Gottwald's government. The
People's Party had always been a minority party,
always a member of coalitions, and the new
leadership thought that it could continue its
traditional role as coalition partner with the
Communist Party. The new Secretary General (also
named Hala) therefore refused to purge the party
organisation, but was quickly dismissed and
replaced by a more willing secretary, A. Pospisil.
After the election in 1948, in which parts of
the country under the People's Party's influence,
had voted solidly against the new National Front,
Pospisil was ordered to dismantle the party
organisation. The party blamed the Catholic
Church for the 'disloyalty' of its members in the
election; the Communist Party took advantage of
this conflict and destroyed them both. In 1950
only 2.3 per cent of People's Party members were
still in public life.

     In Slovakia, where the non-Communists were
in the majority, the purge was even more ruthless
than in the Czech provinces. The Democratic
Party disintegrated and changed its name to the
Slovak Party of Renaissance: top leaders either
escaped abroad or joined the Communist Party.
The latter example was emulated particularly at
the district level, where entire committees joined
the Communist Party. Twenty-two members of the
Slovak National Council were expelled thus
enabling the Communist Party to achieve majority
in that body. The other Slovak Party of Freedom
tried for a time to exploit the upheaval in the
ranks of the Democratic Party and recruit their
members. However, the Communist-dominated Action
Committees of the Slovak National Front promptly
stopped this poaching and the Party of Freedom

once again receded into political insignificance.
By 1950 all the Slovak non-Communist parties
ceased to exist as organised bodies, although
their leaders continued a precarious existence at
the top in order to uphold constitutional fiction.[11]

In the economic sphere the effects of the
coup d'état were incalculable. By 1948
Czechoslovakia had achieved a relatively high
standard of living and was much ahead of all the
East European countries, including the USSR, in
industrial production. On the completion of the
Two Year Plan (1946-48), despite difficulties,
Czechoslovak industry produced slightly more than
in 1937, the last normal year before World War
II. Although in heavy industrial goods
production exceeded by one quarter that of
1937, in consumer goods it still lagged behind
(79.8 per cent). The weakness of Czechoslovak
economy was in agriculture: because of the
drought in 1947 agriculture failed to reach the
pre-war level and foodstuffs had to be imported.
On the whole, however, it seemed clear that the
country would economically prosper.

After the coup d'état all industry was
nationalised with the exception of small private
enterprises which accounted for 15.9 per cent
of industrial production. A new Five Year
Plan was prepared to increase industrial
production to 157 per cent and agricultural
production to 154 per cent of the 1937 level;
a significant rise in the standard of living was
forecast. Rapidly it became evident that the
new Plan was unrealistic; nonetheless, the Plan
was thoroughly discussed in the Planning
Commission, the Communist Party and the National
Assembly, which passed it as a law in October
1948.

From the beginning Czechoslovak Communist
leaders were uncertain about the outcome of the
Five Year Plan and above all about the concrete
forecast of the rise in living standards. They
therefore decided to replace this aim with a less
concrete one, that of establishing socialism in

41

Table 2.1

Kaplan 195

Production per Inhabitant 1948 in Eastern Europe

|  | Bulg. | Hung. | DDR | Pol. | Rom. | USSR | CSR |
|---|---|---|---|---|---|---|---|
| Coal kg. | 18 | 135 | 149 | 9230 | 13 | 831 | 1438 |
| Brown Coal | 580 | 1024 | 5767 | 210 | 171 | 323 | 1912 |
| Electricity | 77 | 221 | 766 | 313 | 95 | 368 | 609 |
| Pig Iron | - | 42 | 10 | 58 | 12 | 76 | 133 |
| Steel | 0.3 | 80 | 16 | 82 | 22 | 103 | 212 |
| Cement | 53 | 36 | 49 | 75 | 41 | 36 | 134 |
| Wool Textile | 0.71 | 2.45 | 0.82 | 1.75 | 0.72 | 0.69 | 3.41 |
| Shoes | - | 0.48 | 0.3 | 0.46 | 0.7 | 0.7 | 4.2 |
| Sugar | 8.5 | 15.7 | 32.9 | 30.5 | 5.2 | 9.2 | 41.9 |
| Butter | 0.1 | 0.9 | 2.3 | 0.9 | 0.1 | 1.6 | 1.9 |

Czechoslovakia, and the precaution was proved right.   J. Goldman, one of the economists most concerned with the preparation of the Plan, enumerated several reasons for its failure. In 1949, shortly before he was arrested and imprisoned, Goldman declared that 'the Plan was an amateurish affair which had many weaknesses and the most fundamental one was that it did not secure raw material supplies, because they were outside Czechoslovakia'.   His criticism showed the folly of planning the unplannable and also implied the failure of the USSR and the Communist East European states to help Czechoslovakia economically.   Thus simultaneously with the Plan Czechoslovakia plunged into an inflation, suffered from shortages of raw materials and consumer goods;   its industrial development proved erratic, uneven and unsatisfactory. Ultimately it had to pay for the ideological and power victory of Communism with living standards.[13]

     In agriculture the decline was similar. Although its performance was not outstanding even before the coup d'état, this was largely due to the drought in 1947.   However, there was an additional political factor which was responsible for this lack of performance:   farmers were afraid of wholesale collectivisation on the Soviet pattern and held back investments.   The Communist Party was aware of these fears   and, since it drew sizeable support from the farmers (mainly from those who had benefited from the land confiscations in 1945-6), attempted to deny these rumours as malicious inventions.   However, the situation changed after the coup, and everybody now expected the party to carry out its ideological pledges and collectivise agriculture. However, the party decided to wait.   Since agriculture in Czechoslovakia was run mainly by small and medium farmers, and these farmers worked in highly developed co-operatives, it seemed reasonable to keep the system as it was and improve it.   The state began to establish and finance huge state farms and encouraged the formation of collective farms to increase land

holdings and production. The Plan was going to
make available capital investments to mechanise
farmers and their co-operatives. Gottwald
intended to delay wholesale collectivisation by
three or more years, and Duris, Minister of
Agriculture, demanded increased investments in
agriculture in the FYP. However, in the autumn
of 1948 there occurred difficulties with purchases
of agricultural produce and the party decided to
solve problems in agriculture ideologically.
In 1949 a forcible campaign of collectivisation
was launched and was fiercely resisted. In some
regions it had to be temporarily suspended, but
by then the party took the resistance as a
political challenge and carried out the
collectivisation drive at the price of disrupting
production. The disruption could not have
come at a more inconvenient moment; with the
erratic performance of industry Czechoslovakia
could not buy as much foodstuffs from abroad as
it had hoped. Henceforth the country suffered
chronic food shortages and bread remained strictly
rationed until 1953.

    Thus between 1948 and 1953 Czechoslovakia
went through the most revolutionary purges and
transformation which were not always for the
better. The new system of government emerged
finally towards the end of Gottwald's term in
power in 1953, and it was almost an exact copy of
that in the USSR. This new 'system' provided
for a strong leadership by one man, and only
Gottwald could work it. Paradoxically Gottwald
was fortunate in that constitutionally and by
tradition Czechoslovakia has always provided for
a strong, one man rule in the Presidency. The
Presidents of Czechoslovakia, Professors Masaryk
and Benes, had great powers at their disposal,
but used them sparingly, in emergencies only.
In June 1948, after his election as President,
Gottwald made it clear that he would be a strong
president; conditions in Czechoslovakia as well
as in the other ideologically allied countries,
above all the USSR, favoured this intention.
Thus in Czechoslovakia Gottwald became a Stalinist
dictator organically: he combined the top party

44

office with the Presidency and from that position
he could quite constitutionally destroy the old
system and create his own.  So he muzzled the
National Assembly (already weakened by the new
electoral law) and then transformed it into a
ceremonial Supreme Soviet.  He appointed a weak
government, consisting mainly of his old political
companions who, while politically skilful and
experienced, could not even hope to administer
and run efficiently Czechoslovakia:  after the
purge of the civil service and its virtual
replacement by party picked amateurs, ministers
were not only decision makers, as before, but also
administrators-civil servants.  This task was
probably above any politician's capacity, so
Gottwald came to their rescue and took all decision
making into his own hands.  He strengthened the
presidential chancellory:  presidential officials
were appointed government ministers, trouble-
shooters, political scientists, top civil
servants and economic managers.  Policy
decisions went to the party preasidium which was
Gottwald again.14

     Perhaps rather surprisingly Gottwald had
less trouble with the state machine than with the
party machine turning them into his personal
instruments of power.  The party secretariat,
led by the capable ... Slansky, tried to seize as
much executive power as it could.  Slansky
himself concentrated on matters of national
security, though he also convinced his fellow
leaders, Gottwald and Zapotocky, of the necessity
of economic planning, collectivisation of
agriculture and administrative reorganisation.
For a short time it seemed that Slansky and the
secretariat would remain in control, especially
after the first steps of the gigantic reforms and
reorganisations resulted in chaos and confusion.
It appeared that Slansky would compete for power
with Gottwald and the secretariat with the
preasidium.  However, on Soviet advice Gottwald
swiftly eliminated Slansky, executing him
ultimately, and the secretariat became a purely
administrative office.

The Communist Party's central committee also
wanted greater powers in the changed circumstances in Czechoslovakia, but in the end had to
content itself with the trappings of power.  It
tried unsuccessfully to assume the role of the
old National Assembly:  it wanted to formulate
and vote party policies which now became state
policies.  The central committee even took to
meeting in the historical Vladislav Hall in the
Prague royal castle, but there its power
stopped.  Like Stalin, Gottwald wanted an
obedient rubber stamp and after purging a few
argumentative members and intimidating the rest
the central committee was allowed to meet and
approve unanimously without debate the leaders'
decisions.  In May 1949 Gottwald convoked the
ninth congress of the Czechoslovak Communist
Party, which most enthusiastically approved all
the changes in Czechoslovakia since the coup
d'état thus legitimising Gottwald's position and
power.  The Communist Party was also reorganised
so as to be "capable of governing":  Soviet
experience had to be utilised so that the
Communist Party of Czechoslovakia finally became
an almost exact copy of the Soviet party.
Gottwald also requested Stalin to send him
experienced Soviet advisers to help with the
reorganisation, especially of security and the
army.  The central committee itself was turned
into a huge bureaucracy:  departments were
established to cover the whole gamut of national
existence and they were responsible and reported
to the leader, Gottwald.  To make quite sure that
the central committee did not usurp too much
power for itself Gottwald convoked its sessions
irregularly:  in 1948, after the coup, it met
three times;  in 1949 twice (to 'elect' the new
leadership);  in 1950 once;  in 1951 three times
and in 1952 once.  Since Gottwald convoked the
meeting of the preasidium-politburo also only
occasionally, the Czechoslovak Communist Party
ceased to be a mass political body subject to its
rules and statutes, and instead became the
Stalinist bureaucratic machine resembling a
political party only externally.  All power
resided in President Gottwald - the party leader,

who maintained himself in power by controlling
the new security *apparat* and the army, managed
for him by Soviet advisors. Practically nothing
was left of the old Czechoslovakia and to infuse
some dynamism into this new Czechoslovakia a
vigorous application of Soviet type of terror
was necessary. As long as Stalin and Gottwald
were alive, it was quite easy to maintain this
system of government, but after their deaths in
March 1953, Czechoslovakia was once again in flux.15

The Rise of the Communist Party

The substitution of the Communist Party for the
previous political system was a difficult task
even for Gottwald with his terror and deadly
purges. In fact Gottwald and the Communist
leaders did not particularly wish the destruction
of the political system. In 1945, on their
return from Moscow, the Communist leaders were
quite sure that they would be able to choose
their own "Czechoslovak way to socialism" and
this in their opinion meant that they would use
the party to conquer power within the Czechoslovak
system and then continue organically "the
building of socialism" in Czechoslovakia with
that system, now only slightly modified.16

Thus, between 1945-48, the Communist Party
of Czechoslovakia aimed at mass membership and
electoral victories. From the end of the war to
the eighth congress in March 1946 the party
succeeded in recruiting over one million members
and emerged from the general election in June
1946 as the largest party in Czechoslovakia.
After the election the drive for new members
continued unabated and by February 1948 there
were some 1,400,000 registered members of the
Communist Party of Czechoslovakia. Then the
victorious coup opened the floodgates and by May
1949 the party contained over two million members
and candidates. More than happy about its
recruitment of members the party leadership
launched a pre-election slogan in the autumn of
1947: it wanted to poll 51 per cent of the vote

in the scheduled election in the spring of 1948.
This was to be the first electoral decisive
victory by any Communist party; the party would
come to power through the ballot box; it would
govern alone and implement its policies unhindered
by any coalition partners. This seemed to be the
the tactic in 1947; however, by February 1948
the Communist Party carried out a 'constitutional'
coup d'état and gained absolute power in this way
rather than through the ballot box. However, the
rapid growth in membership after the coup probably
indicates that the Communist leaders were not
clear about their ultimate aims and still wanted
a decisive majority of the nation to back their
policy in the accepted democratic sense. Only
in September 1948 did the central committee get
down to discussing the post coup flood of new
members and considered steps for stemming it.
It was argued that the social composition of the
Communist Party had so changed by the influx of
new members that a purge became necessary to put
the balance right. Thus as late as September
1948 the party leadership finally realised that
it no longer needed a mass party loosely organised,
but that it would have to be reshaped and its
function changed. It seems very plausible to
suppose that K. Gottwald and the Communist
leadership were so satisfied with the take over
of the Czechoslovak political system that far
from wanting it destroyed they just wanted to
infuse it with their members and otherwise keep
it intact as their way to Communism. This
reasoning was probably at the root of wholesale
admissions into the Communist Party of state
officials (civil servants) and other
administrators who before the coup amounted to
some 5.8 per cent of the overall party membership;
after the coup their numbers more than doubled
(13.6 per cent). It seemed clear that the
Communist Party would make use of existing
political institutions to govern: the presidency,
to which Gottwald was unanimously elected in
June 1948; the coalition government, in which
the Communist Party now had an overwhelming
majority; and the newly elected National Assembly
(parliament), where the party also had a two-third

majority to enable it to vote through any reform
it thought necessary to make Czechoslovakia a
Communist state.[17] However, after his summer
holiday in the Crimea with Stalin, Gottwald came
back to Czechoslovakia a changed man:   evidently
he then was given precise instructions as to the
Czechoslovak Communist system of government.
It appears that Gottwald was ordered to destroy
the Czechoslovak political system and remodel his
party on the Soviet pattern and then substitute
it for the political structures in Czechoslovakia.
If Gottwald found it difficult to perform such
tremendous transformation, Stalin promised him
help in the form of Soviet advisers.   Within six
months Gottwald admitted difficulties and Soviet
advisers were quickly called for, especially in
the field of national security.[18] With their help
Gottwald fused the most powerful office of the
state, the presidency, with that of the party
leader;   he destroyed the government by dissolving
the professional civil service so that
Czechoslovakia ceased to be administered but
was nevertheless ruled by Communist ministers by
means of the party administration.[19] The parliament
voted itself out of existence and the judiciary
system was abolished and replaced by a "class
judiciary".[20] The newly formed departments of the
central committee practically took over the
central government, while the long established
regional, district and local party organisations
took over the local government.   The security
police was started from scratch while the army was
mercilessly purged and then reformed on the Soviet
pattern.   To facilitate this party fusion
Czechoslovakia's administration was 'decentralised'
on 1 January 1949 and regions rather than lands
became the administrative basis.   Schools,
universities, the economy and communication media
were also reshaped and disorganised while the
party's grip on all of them was tightened.

        In order to successfully destroy the
Czechoslovak political system and to exercise
power in the Soviet manner, Gottwald had to
reshape the Communist Party.   After purging it
of 'undesirable' elements' thus incidentally

making sure that it would obey him absolutely. Gottwald put the party apparat in place of the state administration, local government, trade unions, universities, army and security. It is perhaps surprising to see how well he succeeded in this task, for even his successors could not disentangle the party from this power mesh and only in 1968 did the 'regeneration' movement led by the new party leadership begin to cut loose the party from the state; but then it was toppled by foreign intervention.

Before the coup d'état the Communist Party's praesidium was only a loose body: all ministers belong to it ex officio and the secretary general, Slansky, prepared its agenda. It met irregularly and made decisions on immediate political problems facing the party. It undoubtedly endorsed the decision to carry out a coup d'état in February 1948, though detailed decisions were left to individual ministers. It was rather a co-ordinating body which made final overall decisions. After the coup d'état Gottwald, on Soviet advice, transformed this loose body into the ultimate decision making organ of, not only policies, but also power measures and other details. Since the composition of the praesidium remained the same and the body was too large to consider all that it should, it could only mean that Gottwald wanted to keep all the powers of decision to himself as chairman of the praesidium. In April 1945 Gottwald's praesidium consisted of six men only: Slansky, Gottwald's faithful companion and secretary; Kopecky, a demagogic orator who became Minister of Information in the first government of Czechoslovakia; V. Nosek, a trade unionist returning from Britain who also became Minister of the Interior; and two Slovak Communists, Siroky and Smidke, both emerging from the Slovak uprising and therefore unknown quantities. Subsequently Gottwald added to the praesidium J. Smrkovsky, but quickly dropped him (May-June 1945); A. Zapotocky, his most permanent companion; J. Dolansky, a university professor who became his economic and administrative brain; J. Duris,

a Slovak who replaced Smidke; J. Krosn r, another
trade unionist; and M. Svermova, wife of
Gottwald's companion killed in the war, who
became a secretary.  However, when in March 1946
a large praesidium was elected at the Eighth
Congress, Gottwald got round it by forming a
narrow praesidium consisting of people nearest to
him: Konecky, Dolansky, Zapotocky, Slansky and
Siroky, who was the only Slovak willing to listen
to him.  It was this narrow praesidium which took
the decision to carry out the coup d'état in 1948
and it remained in power until June 1948 (with
the exception of Siroky whose duties then took
him to Slovakia), when the Communist Party fused
with the Social Democratic Party.  Apart from
Social Democrats (Erban E. Fierlinger), Gottwald
added to this body a number of Communists in
charge of the demolition of the system:  Nosek
was back;  Kopriva in charge of security;
Svermova secretary;  Frank another secretary;
Duris and Siroky (as Slovaks) thus making it so
large as to be incapable of decision.  In May
1949 the Ninth Congress enlarged it with more
secretaries (G. Bares, V. David) and trade
unionists (Krosnar was back;  G. Kliment acting
secretary of the TUC) who perhaps rightly
deserved to be represented in the supreme organ
of the Communist Party, but only served to destroy
this body.  By then Gottwald had no need for a
representative praesidium;  he had his son-in-law
Cepicka, co-opted in it and then in the closest
co-operation with Cepicka and Zapotocky began to
make decisions on his own.  The praesidium was
no longer convoked to meet and shortly afterwards
was purged and replenished with nonentities
(Novotny, John, Barak).  Zapotocky as Prime
Minister invariably endorsed Gottwald's decisions;
in his devotion he went even as far as to entice
the unsuspecting Slansky, whom Gottwald decided
to liquidate on Soviet advice, to his villa and
then deliver him to the security police.  Cepicka
became Gottwald's troubleshooter internally, and
externally in the Cominform, but how much advice
he could give Gottwald is far from clear.  In the
end Gottwald made absolutely all decisions and the
newly moulded and regenerated party carried them

51

out.

Since the newly established departments of
the central committees were supposed to serve the
praesidium, Gottwald made good use of them. He
had purged and destroyed the secretariat so that
the departments could do so and refer their
problems and decisions directly to him. The
departments encompassed absolutely everything:
the cadre department was responsible for the
selection of Communist leaders and Gottwald put
in its charge, L. Kopriva (Svermova was removed
in 1949) who was also a security expert and member
of the praesidium. He could make sure of
Kopriva in three respects, if he needed to: as
a fellow member of the party's praesidium Gottwald
could impart to him all the instructions that he
cared in that body: as President he checked on
Kopriva's work as Minister of Security and as
party chairman he had Kopriva waiting on him as
head of the cadre department. This system of
checks proved quite watertight and there was a lot
of justification in Kopriva's statement in 1968
when he claimed that he was nothing but a
messenger boy on his leader's errands, who had
stopped work when the errands became too dangerous
even for the errand boy.

Gottwald had also a security department at
his disposal. However, he used it as yet very
little, for security problems were passed on to
Soviet experts, who arrived in 1949, and the
department was staffed by people who were probably
not known to Gottwald personally. Until 1951
the department was headed by J. Svab, who was
M. Svermova's brother, who in turn was secretary
of the central committee. She was widow of Jan
Sverma, Gottwald's companion during the war and a
determined lady who had built up for herself and
her family a cosy niche in the party *apparat*.
Svermova's downfall was followed by Svab's
liquidation and since he was more exposed than
his sister he paid with his life. The department
was taken over by J. Salga, a singularly grey
*apparatchik*, who survived as head the 'distorted'

years of Gottwald's cult, but failed to make a
political career out of this assignment, which was
rather untypical, for even his deputies (O. Papez,
K. Innemann and others) prospered as a result.
Another head, M. Mamula managed to survive even the
cataclictic 1968 without damage and subsequently
consolidated his political position by becoming
First Regional Secretary and central committee
member. Evidently this department, though
ostensibly dealing with army and security matters,
was not as powerful as its designation indicated:
above all security matters were sorted out else-
where, although the department was used, especially
after Gottwald's death, as a screening and
interrogation centre.

All the other departments, and their numbers
varied as they were often reorganised, served
specific purposes; of these the propaganda and
agitation (sometimes ideological) department and
the economic departments were the most important.
The former had to look after communicating party
policies to the Czechoslovak people, especially
after the coup in 1948. However, judging from
its purge in 1949, when G. Bares, one of the central
committee secretaries was removed as head of this
department, Gottwald did not approve of the way the
department was 'selling' his policies. It is also
clear that after 1949 until his death, Gottwald
had little need of this department: Gottwald came
to rely more on the cadre and security departments
than on this communication department. After
Gottwald's death the department recovered somewhat
and was headed by V. Slavik, who became a central
committee secretary and reformist in 1968.
However, the Czechoslovak Communist Party has not
been very successful with this important department
whose heads (Z. Urban, M. Hladik, P. Auersperg,
F. Havlicek, J. Kozel, L. Novotny and V. Bejda)
have proved to be as ineffective as leaders as the
policies their departments were to propagate.
Thus Hladik gave up party propaganda to become
Czechoslovakia's Security Chief, while Kozel
disappeared altogether after the purge in 1969.
The economic department was to supervise and co-
ordinate the Czechoslovak economy, which task had

rapidly become too difficult for the department and it was therefore several times purged by Gottwald. Most of its heads literally rolled (Frejka was executed) as Czechoslovakia's economic performance declined and only in the 1960s was this department used as a springboard for an economic and political career: L. Adamec rose to become Deputy Premier of the Czech Republic in charge of economy; R. Rohlicek, after serving as Federal Minister of Finace, is Deputy Federal Premier and permanent representative with COMECON, while L. Supka is a federal minister in charge of technology and investments. J. Baryl even became secretary of the central committee which should perhaps be considered as the ultimate height to which the work in the department should lead.

It is quite obvious that these departments (and they covered the whole of national life - chemical industry, education, science and health; youth and mass organisation; energy and fuel; industry, transport, services; etc.) were in fact the political substitutes for governmental departments. At a stroke, Gottwald succeeded in transforming his party from a political body into an administrative apparat, and after he had destroyed the state organisation (the civil service, the judiciary, local administration) he substituted the Communist Party network for it. Since Gottwald was the only party leader in control of the party-state apparat, and since he was also President of Czechoslovakia, this fusion could become really effective and total. In fact it was so successfully carried out that his successors could not really undo it. After Gottwald's death President Zapotocky tried to revive the traditional Czechoslovak political institutions without destroying Gottwald's power arrangements and failed. President Novotny hoped to rid himself gradually of the Gottwald apparat and arrangements because they had been compromised by terror; but he was not sure why he should restore the old system. SInce Novotny insisted on retaining the power of the presidency and remaining the party leader, he could not possibl y want to rid himself of the Gottwald system; moreover he insisted on

making the final decisions himself.  On the other
hand, he was prepared to permit his government to
carry out the policies he had approved in any way
they thought fit.  He also allowed a greater say
in policy formulation to the central committee and
the government although he retained the power
and control over central committee departments
and the secretariat.  In the end Novotny was
forced into restoration by economic failures and
since the economy had become part of the political
system economic reforms had also political
consequences.  After his fall in January 1968
all these inconsistencies and shortcomings had been
pinpointed and the new party leadership decided to
cut itself free from the state structures and
administration and concern itself with political
leadership and broad policies, while restoring to
the state structure the old division of power,
checks and balance:  the president was again the
final arbiter of the system in which parliament
legislates and controls, the government governs,
and the judiciary adminsters the law.  All these
'innovations', announced in the new party programme
in April 1968, only began to be implemented when
Czechoslovakia was stopped short and not allowed
to experiment any further in August 1968.  In
1969 numerous reforms reversed the experiments of
1968 but it is far from clear how far they actually
went.

1. J. Mlynsky, Uloha akonich vyboru Narodni fronty pri zajistovani unoroveho vitezstvi, Sbornik historicky, Prague, 1964/12, pp. 132-3; K. Kaplan, Utva.eni generalni linie vystavby socialismu v Ceskoslovensku, Prague, 1966, pp. 23-31.

2. Kaplan, ibid., p. 100.

3. J. Zizka, Unorova politicka krize a statni aparat lidove demokracie, Ceskoslovensky casopis historicky, Prague, 1973/5, pp. 663-7.

4. L. Kalinova, K pounorovym zmenam ve slozeni ridiciho aparatu, Revue dejin socialismu, Prague, 1969/4, pp. 494-5.

5. J. Solc, KSC- vedouci sila budovani CSLA armady socialistickeho typu v letech 1948 az 1955, Historie a vojenstvi, Prague, 1973/2-3, pp. 331-43.

6. A. Neuman, Novy pravni rad v lidove demokracii, Prague, 1952, pp. 50-7.

7. V. Belda, Mocensko-politicke zmeny v CSR po unoru 1948, Revue dejin socialismu, Prague, 1969/2, p. 242.

8. Dejiny a soucastnost, Prague, 1968/8, p. 46; also Zizka, op. cit., p. 674.

9. Dejiny university v Brne, Brno, 1969, pp. 233-83.

10. Kaplan, op. cit., pp. 83-90.

11. V. Pavlicek, Nektere poznamky k cinnosti Narodni fronty v CSR z hlediska systemu vice politickych stran, Prispevky k dejinam KSC, 1963/5, pp. 692-6.

12. Kaplan, op. cit., pp. 193-261; Dr J. Dolansky, Tri leta planovani v lidove demokratickem Ceskoslovensku, Prague, 1949,

a rather pathetic survey of economic
development by the chief planner.

13.   J. Spacil, Nektere vysledky kolektivizace
      na stredni a severni Morave v letech 1952
      az 1953, Prispevky k dejinam KSC, 1967/6,
      pp. 878-904.

14.   Belda, op. cit., p. 241.

15.   M. Caha, M. Reiman, O nekterych otazkach
      vedouci ulohy strany v obdobi budovani
      socialismu v Ceskoslovensku, Prispevky k
      dejinam KSC, Prague, 1962, p. 860.

16.   J. Belda, Ceskoslovenska cesta k socialismu,
      Prispevky k dejinam KSC, 1967/1, p. 17;
      J. Opat, O novou demokracii, Prague, 1966,
      pp. 203-29.

17.   Belda, op. cit., p. 242.

18.   The Czechoslovak Political Trials, 1950-54,
      London, 1971, pp. 76ff.

19.   Kalinova, op. cit., gives impressive figures
      which are supplemented by Zizka.

20.   Handpicked workers were admitted to the law
      faculty at Prague University and began to
      practise their profession even before they
      were given law degrees (Dejiny a soucastnost,
      Prague, 1968/8, p. 46).

# CHAPTER III

## Constitutions and Parliaments

*Constitutions*

Until 9 May 1948 the constitution passed in 1920 was in force in Czechoslovakia. This constitution was based on the legal system and procedures of the defunct Habsburg Monarchy and was then only slightly modified to suit new conditions in the Czechoslovak republic. The proclamation of independence by the National Committee of Prague, on 28 October 1918, was embodied in the constitution. On 14 November 1918, the National Assembly (Parliament) composed of Czech members of the Imperial Parliament and of co-opted members, passed a provisional constitution, which in 1919 was twice amended (Acts 138 and 271), but remained in force until 1920 when a new constitution was drafted and approved by the National Assembly.

On the instruction from the President of Czechoslovakia the Ministry of the Interior formed a committee of experts and started work on the draft; the ministry team, of course, consulted freely with political parties and other bodies. On 10 December 1919 it passed its proposals to the special constitutional committee of the National Assembly. This committee discussed the draft for three months at fifteen sessions and prepared its own report to be submitted to the National Assembly alongside with the ministry draft: the Social Democratic members also submitted their minority report. The Assembly then discussed the draft and three reports, and finally accepted them all. On 29 February 1920 the constitution was passed by the Assembly and became law on 6 March 1920.

The constitution was a mixture of several constitutions, but as a basic law it certainly

satisfied the need of the new Czechoslovak state.
Still in 1920 several of its chapters were re-
drafted and improved by several amendments passed
by the Assembly in the form of constitutional
laws, but otherwise it remained in force without
substantial modification until the war in 1939.
The constitution made Czechoslovakia a unitary
state:  the Czech and Slovak provinces were
governed from Prague while Ruthenia became
autonomous.  The President was the head of state
as well as Commander-in-Chief of the armed
forces;  he had great administrative and executive
powers.  He was elected not by popular vote but
by the two chambers, the senate and the chamber
of deputies, of the Czechoslovak Parliament
(National Assembly).  Parliament was elected
directly and secrectly for a period of six years
(the senate for eight).  Political parties
competed for the votes freely by submitting to
the voters lists of candidates.  The President
appointed a government which commanded a majority
in the chamber of deputies, and dismissed it
when it lost the confidence of the lower chamber.
The system was nicely balanced, each institution
checking the other and throughout the existence
of the First Republic (1918-39) it worked
reasonably well.  Basic freedoms were guaranteed
in the constitution and existed in practice
within the system.  However, the Czechoslovak
political system also had several weaknesses:
too many parties competed for power and
constitutional provisions for the protection of
minorities seemed to work less satisfactorily.
In the end the latter problem brought about
external intervention which resulted in the
destruction of Czechoslovakia and its occupation
by Hitler's Germany.

    All constitutional liberties and rights were
suspended in 1938 and the political system was
all but destroyed by the Germans, during the war
1939-45.  The post-war system was radically
different.  Although the 1920 constitution was
in force even after May 1945 when Czechoslovakia
was finally liberated and commenced its independent
life, President Benes, as constitutional head, made

many important amendments to it. Thus in the
form of presidential decrees Dr Benes abolished
the upper chamber, the senate, established purely
elective local government, set up new courts,
nationalised a greater part of industry as well
as disbanding all political parties which
collaborated with the enemy during the war. In
fact Czechoslovakia went into an election in
June 1946 so that the resulting parliament
(Constitutional National Assembly) could draft
and approve a new constitution.

A new political organisation was created,
the National Front, a sort of coalition of the
parties allowed to participate in the new system,
where policies were discussed and agreed to. At
first all the renewed political institutions
were worked by appointed people, but in 1946 after
the election the new system became representative.
The political parties were proportionately
represented, not only in parliament and government, but also in local government.

After the election in 1946 the National
Assembly immediately set up a constitutional
committee composed proportionately of all the
parties represented in the Assembly, which
immediately began to draft the new constitution.
Although the drafting was held up on several
occasions when the parties could not agree the
draft was almost completed when in February 1948
the Communist Party seized power through a coup
d'état. Curiously the Communist Party did not
substantially amend the draft nor pass it
through the intimidated (and to a certain extent
truncated) National Assembly; instead it waited
for a new election, resignation of the President
and only then had it passed unanimously by the
newly elected Assembly. Henceforth the legal
basis of life in Czechoslovakia became the so-
called May Constitution of 1948.

Evidently during the drafting in the years
1945-8 constitutional experts and the constitutional committee of the Assembly had to face and
resolve many difficult points. Thus only a

fraction of the 1920 constitution corresponded to
reality: Paragraph 5 concerning Ruthenia was
invalid, for this province was ceded to the USSR.
Paragraphs 6 and 7 concerning Slovakia were
largely out of date: the Slovak National
Council which established itself in Slovakia
after the uprising in 1944 took over powers so
far reserved for the central government (Chapter
2). Paragraphs concerning the senate, age
qualifications of electors and candidates as well
as the electoral court were inapplicable. With
the abolition of the senate, the election of the
President had to be modified: Paragraph 80
dealing with the central government had to be
changed, too. Paragraph 86 concerning state
administration became invalid, when national
councils were set up, and Chapter 6 concerned
with the protection of minorities became
superfluous, after almost all the minorities had
been deported and expelled from the country.
However, Chapter 5 containing rights and freedoms
of the citizens was largely modified. The
greatest problem the constitution had to
resolve was the position of Slovakia in the
republic, and the position of political parties
which were involved in all the three classical
components of the political system, the
legislative, executive and judiciary.

The resutling May Constitution was certainly
a Communist one, but it was not of the 'higher'
Soviet type: it simply established another
hybrid Czechoslovak system, the People's
Democratic principle was the key to it: the
people were the source of all power and power
(legislative, executive and judiciary) belonged
to the people. The people governed themselves
through elective representative organs (national
committees - soviets - parliament and government).
The basic constitutional principle of the people's
democracy was further developed. The Communist
Party, by assuming the leading role, in effect
cancelled the democratic principles of
representation and division of power.

The Communist Party wanted the constitution

to reflect not only the status quo in Czechoslovakia, but also to serve as a source of future
legislation, a 'critical criterion' of the legal
system as well as one of the power means for the
democratisation of the legal system;   it no
longer wanted the constitution to be the basic
law of the state, from which all the laws were
derived.   It was to be a political document, a
people's charter as well as a declaration of
political intention.   A declamative part was
added to the introduction which was purely
ideological and extolled the type of dictatorship
of the Czechoslovak proletariat the Communist
Party established after the coup d'état.   Moreover, the basic articles which followed this
introductory declamation shortly became
theoretical, too;   the third part of the
constitution which contained descriptive norms
of the political system was also out of date by
the end of 1948.   While the Communist Party
thought that it achieved its revolution in
February 1948 and proclaimed it solemnly in this
constitution, it had actually only just embarked
on it.   Thus, apart from its declamative parts,
the 1948 constitution sorted out nothing and was
out of date practically at the same time as it
became law.

In 1968 when all the past was subject to
criticism, Communist constitutional experts tore
this constitution to pieces.   The fusion of
powers which the constitution allowed by upholding
the principle of the Communist Party leadership
in all affairs, was blamed for the excesses of
the period of the cult of personality 1949-53.
It was argued that by allowing the offices of
party leader and of President to fuse, it enabled
President Gottwald to become Czechoslovakia's
Stalin with all it meant.   Gottwald transformed
the government into the civil service, making all
policy decisions himself and took away from the
National Assembly its powers of control.   In
this way he could exercise power and commit
excesses without any restraint.   In addition,
the constitution also failed to sort out the
nationality problem:   it gave a measure of autonomy

with its legislative assembly, the Slovak National Council but no real executive, and since the Council was weakened as was its Czechoslovak counterpart in Prague, the National Assembly, Slovakia was in fact ruled as it had been previously, directly from Prague.

Although numerous objections were raised against this constitution immediately after Gottwald's death in 1953 and especially after 1956, the successors of Gottwald, Zapotocky and Novotny, tried to cling to this 'basic law' and above all to its practice, especially after 1957, when once again the office of the party leader and President were fused. The restless Slovaks were purged, though not liquidated as was the case before. In the end, however, Novotny gave in to pressure, and in 1960 produced another constitution which was to tidy up Czechoslovak problems and at the same time proclaim the Czechoslovak republic a socialist state a par with the USSR.

It was obvious that by 1960 the 1948 constitution, even in its descriptive parts, did not correspond to Czechoslovak reality, so even constitutional experts saw a need for revisions. However, no one saw an urgent need for a new constitution. This was rather a political demand by President Novotny who reasoned that the new socialist constitution would enhance his international reputation and standing. Thus in the end the self-proclaimed fact that socialism was established in Czechoslovakia was the only innovation in this constitution. Since the Czechoslovak experts had to explain why they did not copy the Soviet constitution, they argued that socialism in Czechoslovakia developed in a special way and this accounted for the differences. The President remained the all powerful figure in Czechoslovakia, not the titular head of the other Communist states, and this ideological excuse pacified Novotny especially since he could clearly see that the other Czechoslovak 'differences' would not work in practice. The constitutional experts tried, for example, to restore some of the powers of the National Assembly as "this was a feature of the Czechoslovak revolutionary tradition"; the Slovak problem was, if anything, exacerbated since Slovakia lost the remaining ministries and the Slovak National Council was still further weakened by this change.

According to expert opinion this constitution concentrated on a restatement of citizen rights and duties, as these had been most abused in the recent past, despite the 1948 constitution. The 1960 constitution no longer contained articles prohibiting the misuse of liberties, but did contain many categorical rights and duties. The difficulty was that these rights and duties were not formally defined, had often no legal basis nor institutional backing for their implementation. Society as such was expected to decide when these constitutional rights and duties were infringed and that was obviously impractical. Moreover, the legal position of the Communist Party was embedded in the constitution itself. It was no longer understood that the Communist Party as the strongest element of the National Front ruled the country. Similar to the Soviet formula, the Communist Party became the leading power in society and in the state (Chapter 1, Paragraph 4) and was supreme in everything. Although Paragraph 6 spoke of the National Front as the political body of all workers from town and country led by the Communist Party, this was no longer the National Front coalition but an association of social and other organisations. A little paradoxically the Communist Party continued to share power with four other political parties, although these parties were not mentioned in the constitution and were not allowed to represent different interests and policies from those of the leading Communist Party. They simply represented social groups in politics - the Czech Socialist Party supposedly represented the Czech intelligentsia; the (Catholic) People's Party represented Catholic farmers (individual and collectivised) etc. In any case, this particular constitutional arrangement was

contrary to that in the Soviet Union, where no
organised political bodies were admitted into the
ruling coalition of the Communist Party and the
non-party citizens.  Thus it largely invalidated
the declamative part of the constitution which
proclaimed Czechoslovakia a socialist state a par
with the USSR, or at least made this claim highly
implausible.

However imperfect this constitution turned
out to be, it would have satisfied another
generation of Czechs and Slovaks had it not been
for the crisis in 1968 through which the
Communist Party of Czechoslovakia passed.  As a
result of this crisis the leadership of the
Communist Party was removed and replaced by
another, which then vehemently attacked the 1960
constitution.  In the action programme of the
Communist Party approved on 5 April 1968, the
constitution was practically demolished and
instructions were given to commence work on a
new one.  Thus all the rights and duties of the
Czechoslovak citizens were to be clearly defined
and guaranteed by institutions, legal or
otherwise.  The National Front became again
a coalition body where political parties acted
as partners and the leading role of the Communist
Party was defined as moral leadership.  Above
all the new constitution was to resolve for ever
and equitably the Slovak minority problem.
However, before the new constitution could even
be drafted, the occupation of Czechoslovakia
by the Warsaw Pact armies stopped work on it and
in the end it was not accomplished.

Instead the National Assembly passed a
large number of constitutional amendments and
they form the basis of the present constitution.
Act 100/1968 cancelled Chapters 3-6 of the old
constitution and transformed Czechoslovakia into
a federal republic consisting of two equal Czech
and SLovak republics.  Act 143/1968 defined and
formalised this federation while laws 144/1968
regulated the position of the nationalities within
the federation.  Act 10/1969 established the
State Council of Defence and Act 126/1970 defined

federal powers and administration, thus completing the transformation of Czechoslovakia. Despite the interruption caused in the drafting of the constitution by the occupation of the country, Czechoslovakia, alone in the Communist world remained constitutionally in a unique position: it does not have one constitution, but five constitutional laws which form its basis. In addition many laws were passed by the Federal Assembly which have the force of constitutional amendments and are considered as parts of the constitution.

According to this composite constitution Czechoslovakia is a socialist state because it is based on the power of the workers, farmers and intellectuals led by the Communist Party. It is also socialist because all its economy is nationalised and it is a member of the Warsaw Pact and the Communist international system. The state is a republic headed by a President; both Czech and Slovak republics form the Federal Republic of Czechoslovakia. The President is elected by the Federal Assembly, which is a federal parliament consisting of two chambers: the People's Chamber elected directly, and the Nations Chamber consisting of equal numbers of Czech and Slovak deputies. Contrary to other Communist countries, the President is an individual and not a collective; the political system is multiple - political parties take part in it although they all recognise the leading role of the Communist Party.

The basis of the state is formed by representative institutions elected by the people. The Federal Assembly is elected in parliamentary elections which are direct, secret and whose candidates are selected by the National Front. Its special position in the system was abolished in 1970 after a law passed in 1968 was repealed. Each republic has also separate legislative bodies, the National Councils, which appoint and control republican executive governments, as does the Federal Assembly on the federal level. Local government bodies are also elected, but have administrative services (civil service) to carry out their policies.

The President and the State Council of Defence are responsible for national security and defence; the former is Commander-in-Chief and declares war after consultation with the council and on approval by the Federal Assembly. Internal security is assured by the Corps of National Security (police) which is subordinated to the Ministry of the Interior and whose position is constitutionally undefined, being sufficiently explicit. Other bodies securing internal order are also left out of the constitution: the People's Militia, an 'instrument of defence for the working class'; Fire Brigades and the Voluntary Guard of Public Order. The ultimate control over public order and observance or infringements of law belongs to the procuracy and courts which are clearly defined in the various federal laws.

This new constitution transformed Czechoslovakia completely and was in many ways a break with the past. However, since 1968, while Czechoslovakia is formally completely different from what it was before, many of the past practices have been resumed after 1970. Thus it will be pertinent to consider the legislature first, as it is the core of the Czechoslovak political system, and point out its unique aspects as well as putting it into a correct perspective.


*Parliaments*


Preliminary Remarks

Since its inception in 1918 the National Assembly, or Parliament, has been the most important political institution in Czechoslovakia. In all the constitutions of Czechoslovakia (1920, 1948 and 1960) the National Assembly is described as the supreme representative body in which national sovereignty resides (Article 39, Paragraph 1). Apart from its unique legislative powers it also has great controlling powers, and above all elects the head of state, the President, as well as the Supreme Court judges. By tradition it is the vehicle to power: politicians of all parties enter parliament in order to achieve power, either in the executive (central government) or in the presidency. It is curious to note that the Communist politicians after their victorious coup in 1948, continued to respect and carry on with this tradition. Thus, before the coup, Communist deputies were also members of the party's central committee; the ministers whom the party chose from the deputies were automatically members of the party praesidium. After the coup in the 1948 election there was a sudden influx of Communist leaders into parliament (especially those who had no chance of being elected in the conditions of pre-coup Czechoslovakia): A. Novotny, the future party leader and President, finally got elected. But other leaders also made their entry into 'politics': in December 1948 J. Hendrych entered the Assembly in a bye-election, followed by H. Leflerova, V. Knap, A. Dubcek, etc. In subsequent parliaments every really ambitious Communist politician made sure that he was elected to the Assembly, even though after the years of personality cult (1949-53) this body politic appeared fairly battered (some 150 members were purged): O. Homola re-emerged, V. Skoda, B. Cakrtova, C. Hruska, J. Sejna, M. Vecker, O. Simunek, L. Stoll, R. Barak, V. Krutina, V. Kolar, V. Janko, P. Majlink, R. Cvik, S. Kodaj, J. Lorincz, V. Litvaj, K. Savel, I. Rendek, and R. Strechaj got elected. In 1960 most of the reform leaders finally made the Assembly: V. Koucky, V. Prchlik, B. Kucera (the liberal leader), L. Strougal, K. Polacek, B. Lomsky, A. Polednak, D. Kolder, O. Cernik, J. Lenart, E. Pepich, V. Bilak and others. Almost all the leaders of the 1968 reform movement became members of parliament in 1964, and their successors made sure that they were added to this body after the

purges 1969-71 or in the 1971 election. President
L. Svoboda has been a member of all the parliaments
since 1945.

Thus the unique and powerful position of the
Assembly in the political life of Czechoslovakia
was recognised even by the leaders of the
Communist Party, who after all served their
political apprenticeship in this body. This
realisation was expressed in the negative sense
by the destructive effects of the personality
cult, during the years 1948-53, on the National
Assembly. In these long years the party was
'afraid' of this institution, and purged it
ruthlessly. Then it tried to muzzle it, and
transform it into a perfect replica of the
Supreme Soviet in the USSR. Though it overtly
destroyed its competitive electoral basis in
1948, as well as procedural processes, and its
committee system in 1950, it nevertheless failed
to transform the Assembly into a Supreme Soviet:
it remained a truncated Czechoslovak Parliament.
Immediately after President Gottwald's death the
Communist Party decided to revive this important
political institution, which still seemed to have
a place within the new system. The problem
was how to resurrect it? In 1953 President
Zapotocky tried to infuse new life into it by
personally attending its plenary sessions. In
1954 A. Novotny hoped that the election would
revive the body. In December 1954 the central
committee sought to achieve this by means of
instructions to members of parliament, but they
proved insufficient. In 1960, after some
administrative reforms and a new constitution,
the Communist Party made new decisions which
were to 'deepen socialist democracy' and increase
the role of the National Assembly (central
committee decisions of 13-14 January 1960 and
7-8 April 1960). However, these decisions still
had no required effect. A public debate ensued
as to the best way in which the Assembly should
be revived: in 1962 the members of parliament
themselves publicly discussed the new and improved
methods of their work (RP 16 February 1962).
But visible improvements only came after the 1964

70

election.  In May of that year the central
committee finally decided on substantial changes
in the working of the Assembly and on the
restitution of its many controls.  Henceforth
it revived incredibly rapidly and came back full
circle into its own during the short hectic
months of 1968.  Altough after the occupation
of Czechoslovakia in August 1968 the National
Assembly was purged and its political status
slightly downgraded, the Federal Assembly of 1971
still retained greater powers and prestige than
those Assemblies in the period 1948-68.

Structurally, the Communist Party changed
the National Assembly only marginally between
1948-68;  great structural changes did occur
after the federal law had been passed (Act 143/
1968).  Thus the uni-cameral Assembly established
in 1945 remained unchanged after the coup in
1948 until 1949, when certain powers and
importance of the plenary session were curtailed
in favour of the Speaker and the praesidium, as
in the USSR.[1]  Within this structure only the
praesidium and the few remaining committees did
really work, while the plenary session became
largely formal.  In 1964 only a major shift
occurred back to the pre-1949 arrangements:  the
praesidium's powers were weakened, the committees
still further strengthened and consequently the
plenary session became lively and important again.
Throughout 1968 this shift in emphasis was fully
maintained, but soon structural changes brought
about new and unprecedented conditions.

Throughout 1945-68 the Slovak province of
Czechoslovakia had its own provincial parliament
(Slovenska narodni rada), but because of fears
of separatism this body never really prospered
and rapidly became an insignificant appendix of
the National Assembly.  In 1960 its existence
reached its lowest depth when its executive branch
(Poverenictvo) was abolished.  However, in 1968
it was not only resurrected but also given new
powers, so that it became a real legislative and
controlling body of SLovak autonomy which it was
supposed to be from the very beginning in 1944.

71

In the federal re-organisation of Czechoslovakia, the Slovaks also achieved another type of equality with the Czechs by having a second chamber added to the Federal Assembly. The Nation's Chamber consists of an equal number of Czech and Slovak deputies and has a power of veto. In addition each republic (Czech and Slovak) has its own legislative body which passes republican laws and controls its own republican executive.

It is curious to note that the new federal system, and above all the legislative arrangements, though arising out of the reforms in 1968, departs almost completely from the historical arrangements and customs in Czecho-slovakia and closely resembles the Soviet system.


Electoral Laws

One factor that made the various Assemblies such a powerful institution was the laws which governed their elections. The Czechs and Slovaks had a long though differing historical experience as far as electoral laws were concerned. Since 1907 (Act 15, 26 February 1907) the Czechs could elect their representatives to the central parliament (Reichsrat) on the basis of universal suffrage, directly and secretly. Only two minor qualifications prevented this Act from being fully democratic: every male over twenty-four could vote provided he had been a resident in a constituency for over one year; the major one was that women had no voting rights. On the other hand the Slovaks only got comparable voting rights after the collapse of Austria-Hungary in 1918.

Electoral arrangements were basically regulated in the Constitution of 1920 and in a series of Acts which modified certain procedures. In 1919 (Act 663) permanent electoral lists in all communes were made compulsory; twice every year these lists were made public so that objections could be lodged or amendments made. Act 44 in 1920 only slightly completed Act 663.

Table 3.1

National Assembly 1945-49

```
National Assembly ──────────────────────── N.A.
       (300)                                Office
         |
 Plenary Session
         |
     Speaker
         |
   Praesidium
         |
   Committees
     (6-11)
         |
     Members
      (300)


Slovak National Council ───────────────── S.N.C.
         |                                 Office
   Praesidium
         |
     Speaker
         |
  Plenary Session
         |
   Committees
         |
     Members
      (100)
```

Acts 123 and 208 of 1920 regulated the election of
the National Assembly (parliament).  (Only slight
changes to these two Acts were effected in 1925
and 1935.)  The bi-cameral Assembly was elected
on the basis of universal suffrage by all (male
and female) citizens of Czechoslovakia over the
age of twenty-one (over twenty-six for the Senate)
who resided in a constituency over three months.
Thus vagrants, but also bankrupts and other

73

convicted citizens were (or could be) disqualified from the vote.  In 1927 (Act 56) members of the armed forces and gendarmerie were also disqualified.  The other qualifications in 1920 were that candidates for the lower chamber had to be thirty years of age (for the senate forty-five) and had to be citizens of Czechoslovakia for at least three years (for the senate ten years).

Elections were organised by the Ministry of the Interior.  The Ministry had to announce the election date at least twenty-eight days beforehand; electoral lists were displayed for fourteen days and candidates had to be nominated sixteen days before the election.  The Ministry worked through electoral commissions:  (1) local ones which compiled electoral lists;  (2) district ones which organised the ballot and whose members were representatives of the parties or groups taking part in the election;  (3) regional ones which supervised and amended electoral lists and checked results;  and (4) a central commission appointed by the Minister (political parties had twelve members on it) which supervised the whole operation and announced final results.

There were no single constituencies but representation was proportionate.  Every party or group received proportionate representation based on its vote.  The defeated candidates in a given electoral district became substitutes in the order of poll.  If a seat fell vacant, the next candidate on the list became automatically member.  On the other hand members of parliament were not directly responsible to the electorate. The Constitution of 1920 (Paragraph 22) made members independent and they could not be recalled by their voters.

This perhaps complicated but rather fair system worked satisfactorily throughout the existence of the Republic of Czechoslovakia, 1918-39.  A constitutional court which made final decisions about elections was rarely in action and overall final results were never

questioned.  In 1925 some twenty-nine parties
and groups competed in the general election, in
1929 nineteen, and in 1935 sixteen.  Throughout
this period the Czechoslovak Agrarian Party
emerged as the largest political party, with the
exception of 1920 when the undivided Social
Democratics won the election.  The Communist
Party consistently polled between 10-13 per cent
of the total vote, but never joined the ruling
coalition which consisted of the Agrarian,
Social Democrats, Liberals and Christian
Democrats.  During the war 1939-45 no election
had taken place.  After the war parliament was
urgently required and was therefore elected on an
extraordinary basis.  President Benes issued a
decree (No. 47) which had the force of a
constitutional Act:  it lowered age limits
(eighteen for voters and twenty-one for
candidates), abolished the senate and prescribed
an emergency indirect election.  Local electors
were elected (one per 200 - in Slovakia one per
500) who in turn elected land electors (Bohemia,
Moravia, Slovakia) and the land electors finally
elected members of parliament and their
substitutes.  This Provisional National
Assembly was elected in August 1945 and passed an
electoral law (Act 67) on 11 April 1946 which
regulated the election on 26 May 1946.  This Act
was largely based on the pre-war laws and only
aimed at slightly simplifying the system:  the
senate was definitely abolished and only four
political parties were allowed to compete.  The
age regulations of the Presidential decree were
incorporated in this Act.  Under this system the
Communist Party became the largest single party
and polled some 38 per cent of the total vote.
No opposition party was permitted and the four
competing parties ruled in a coalition called the
National Front.

     After the coup d'état in February 1948 new
electoral arrangements were introduced in the
Constitution passed in May 1948.  Though four
political parties still continued to compete, the
system was considerably simplified.  The National

Front became responsible for the nomination of candidates not the political parties as previously, and there was only one list of candidates for which to vote, that of the National Front in which the Communist Party obtained a disproportionate majority based on the successful coup d'état. No opposition candidates were allowed to stand, but despite additional restrictions (no secret of vote) some 20 per cent of voters voted against the National Front in 1948. This imperfect solution (from the Communist point of view) was not put to another test while President Gottwald was alive. When the necessity for another election was felt, new laws were passed; they brought about the contemporary arrangements (Acts 26 and 27 in 1954, new provisions in the Constitution of 1960, Act 34 in 1964, Act 113 in 1967, and finally Act 43 in 1971).

For the first time in the history of Czechoslovakia all elective assemblies and organs were elected for a period of five years. Though the socialist Constitution of 1960 made provisions for a four year period, this has now been changed. The reason for this change seemed logical: since the Communist Party was acknowledged as the leading force in politics, it seemed appropriate that every election should follow party congresses which meet every five years. The party congress not only endorses past policies, but also formulates future ones: thus every future parliament will also have its policies prepared in advance. Every future election will be 'fought' on a Communist Party programme.

Many of the traditional features of the electoral system were retained: every citizen of Czechoslovakia over eighteen (candidates twenty-one) must participate in an election if he appears on electoral lists. Persons disqualified are the mentally ill or people in jail, or otherwise legally deprived. The differences from the pre-war system are in the process for the nomination of candidates. The

1948 innovation is in force: the National Front, which is an electoral bloc under the leadership of the Communist Party combines other parties and social organisations and is responsible for nominations. Thus even persons not belonging to any party can be nominated by the National Front as candidates and elected. The choice of candidates is made in electoral districts by district National Fronts which then present the picked candidates to the electors and register them with the Czech and Slovak National Fronts. Candidates thus selected are elected by the voters. Electoral commissions at all levels are elected by the corresponding National Fronts and not by representative bodies themselves as during the recent past. The Czech and Slovak National Fronts finalise the choice of candidates, when several nominations are made.

The election for the National (Federal) Assembly is by single constituencies and therefore candidates have to be selected beforehand, as no opposition is permitted. Though local elections take place simultaneously with the parliamentary election, more complicated rules apply: communes of up to 300 inhabitants elect councils of 9; 600 = 11; 1,500 = 17; 10,000 = 40; 20,000 = 60; 50,000 - 80; above 50,000 - 85. District administration is also elected - 80,000 inhabitants elect a 60-member council; above 80,000, 80-member councils: the regional councils elect at least 80-member councils. Constituencies for the bi-cameral Federal Assembly (Peoples and Nations Assemblies) are announced by the praesidium of the Federal Assembly at least sixty days before the election. The praesidia of the Czech and Slovak National Councils similarly form their constituencies. For the Peoples Assembly there are 200 constituencies and for the Nations Assembly 150 (75 in the Czech Republic and 75 in the Slovak Republic). For the Czech National Council there are 200 constituencies, while for the Slovak one only 150. Constituencies contain approximately the same number of electors with the exception of

constituencies of the Nations Assemblies, in which
the Slovak representation is elected approximately
by one-third of the Czechs.  Electoral
commissions appointed by the corresponding
National Fronts organise the election at all
levels;  the central electoral commission of the
National Front is the highest and final authority.

Participation in the election is "morally"
binding and everyone must cast his vote in person.
He can either cast his vote directly, i.e. without
any change; or he can cross out any candidate he
does not approve of, in a room apart, specially
provided for this purpose in order to preserve
the secrecy of choice.  Candidates are elected if
they poll more than one half of the votes.
Elected members are responsible directly to their
voters and can be recalled for various specified
reasons by their electors.  The corresponding
National  Front makes proposals in this respect
after testing public opinion at public meetings.
Members can resign.

The Federal arrangements in Czechoslovakia
required five new Acts to regulate the electoral
system:  Act 44 made provisions for the election
of the Federal Assembly.  Acts 53 and 54 regulated
the elections in the Czech and Acts 55 and 56 in
the Slovak Republics.


Elections:  1948, 1954, 1960, 1964, 1971

Election 1948

After the coup d'état the Communist Party of
Czechoslovakia had no need to woo the electorate
to sanction its political takeover in February
1948.  Seemingly this approval and legitimisation
came from the Constitutional Assembly, where all
political parties were represented and approved
the new government by 230 votes to 70 abstentions.
Subsequently the Congresses of Trades Unions and
the Peasant Commissions, gave them the social
approval which they also needed.  It speaks for

the post-war system and historical tradition that
the Communist Party decided after a decisive
victory to submit itself to the uncertain outcome
of an election ordeal.

At first the praesidium of the Communist
Party which now made all political decisions was
inclined to make use of the existing electoral
procedures and were convinced that they would win
most decisively.  Thus in March 1948 it seemed
that in the coming election the four Czech and
four Slovak parties would put up separate lists of
candidates and that the Communist Party of
Czechoslovakia would obtain between 65-70 per
cent of the votes (on 15 March the estimate was
75 per cent overall).  The difficulty these
estimates presented to the Party praesidium was
that they varied widely from region to region and
in some provinces, Moravia and particularly
Slovakia, could not be guaranteed at all.  Thus
the Bohemian regions of Karlovy Vary and Usti put
their estimates as high at 90 per cent, Mlada
Boleslav and Liberec 85 per cent, while the rest
of Bohemia 75 per cent.  After long hesitation
and probably in view of the uncertainties in
Moravia and Slovakia, the praesidium decided that
parties would not present their individual lists
of candidates but would all combine and put forward
a united National Front list.  The decision was
made public on 5 April 1948 and four days later
it was endorsed by the party's central committee
which prior to the meeting had favoured the
election advocated by the regions.

Once the decision was made it became a
foregone conclusion that the Communist Party would
score an overwhelming majority.  The National
Front which was no longer a coalition body but a
cadre body which the party absolutely controlled,
would nominate candidates and thus determine the
composition of parliament.  However, apart from
this innovation, no great changes were planned and
the Communist Party and other parties which
continued to exist after the coup participated in
elections as a coalition.  The immediate problem
was to make sure that no significant numbers of

voters cast their vote against the National Front
candidates. On the very date of the election
announcement it became obvious that there would
be electoral difficulties in the Ostrava and
Olomouc regions; in these regions as well as in
Slovakia which the Communist Party hardly
controlled at all, it seemed that a massive vote
against the National Front would be registered.
The party therefore decided to make it as
difficult as possible for its opponents.
Election procedures were tightened up: instead
of marking their ballot papers behind a screen,
electores were 'advised' to vote 'publicly' and
cast their votes in front of the election
commissions, without availing themselves of the
privacy of the screen. Tremendous organisational
efforts went into the campaign, some 6,924 pre-
election meetings were organised at which new
procedures were explained: thus the voters were
being subtly or less subtly intimidated into
voting for the National Front. The election took
place on 30 May 1948 and the results proved most
interesting. Some 6.5 per cent of voters failed
to cast their votes, which was more than ever
before, since Czechoslovak citizens were under
legal obligation to vote. These abstentions
were obviously a protest vote. The white votes
amounted to some 770,000, which was 10.7 per cent
of the electorate. As predicted, 228 communes
voted against the National Front by more than
50 per cent. Of these 177 (84 per cent) had
previously been controlled by the Catholic Peoples
Party. The National Front scored nevertheless
an overwhelming victory and polled some 89.3 per
cent of the vote cast. On this united list of
candidates seven political parties presented
themselves for election to parliament. But the
party representation was fixed in the most
arbitrary way by the praesidium of the National
Front which compiled lists of candidates on the
instructions of the Communist Party praesidium.
The Communist Party had 215 members of parliament
(52 of them from Slovakia), when previously, in
1946, it had 114 members only. In this parliament
1948-54 it had a two-third majority (300 members
were elected) and thus could constitutionally carry

Table 3.2

General Election for the Constitutional National Assembly 26 May 1946

| Party | Votes Polled | Percentage | Number of Seats |
|---|---|---|---|
| Communist Party of Czechoslovakia<br>Komunisticka strana Ceskoslovenska | 2,205,697 | 31.05 | 93 |
| Communist Party of Slovakia<br>Komunisticka strana Slovenska | 489,596 | 6.89 | 21 |
| Czechoslovak Peoples Party<br>Ceskoslovenska strana lidova | 1,111,000 | 15.64 | 46 |
| Czechoslovak Social Democratic Party<br>Ceskoslovenska socialni demokracie | 855,538 | 12.05 | 37 |
| Czechoslovak National Socialist Party<br>Ceskoslovenska strana narodne socialisticka | 1,298,980 | 18.29 | 55 |
| Labour Party (Slovakia)<br>Strana prace | 50,079 | 0.71 | 2 |
| Democratic Party (Slovakia)<br>Demokraticka strana | 999,622 | 14.07 | 43 |
| Freedom Party (Slovakia)<br>Strana slobody | 60,195 | 0.85 | 3 |

continued

81

Blank Votes
Opposition votes                    32,117        0.45

–

Source:  Prirucni slovnik k dejinam KSC, Vol. 2, Prague, 1964, p. 971.

Table 3.3

General Election of the National Assembly 30 May 1948

|  | Czech Provinces | Slovak Provinces | Total | Percentage |
|---|---|---|---|---|
| Registered Voters | 6,025,464 | 1,897,359 | 7,922,823 | – |
| Valid Votes | 5,447,383 | 1,751,383 | 7,198,766 | – |
| National Front | 4,920,898 | 1,503,836 | 6,424,734 | 89.25 |
| Blank Votes (opposition) | 526,485 | 247,547 | 774,032 | 10.75 |
| Invalid Votes | 200,792 | 19,695 | 220,487 | – |
| Abstentions | 377,289 | 126,281 | 503,570 | – |

Source:  Prirucni slovnik k dejinam KSC, Vol. 2, Prague, 1964, p. 971.

Table 3.4

Election 1948:  Party Representation

Communist Party of Czechoslovakia (KSC)          215

Communist Party of SLovakia (KSS)                  -

Czech Socialist Party (CSS)                        23

Czech Peoples Party (CSL)                          23

Czech Social Democratic Party (CSD)                23

Slovak Revival Party (SSO)                         12

Slovak Freedom Party (SSS)                          4

Source:  J. Vesely, Kronika unorovych dnu 1948,
         Prague, 1957, p. 219.

---

out any reform, or even abolish the system, if it
wished so.  The three Czech parties were
ungenerously given a block of 23 members each.
The Socialist Party's representation was thus
halved (1946 - 55 members).  The Catholic Peoples
Party and the Slovak Democratic Party also
suffered substnatial losses (in 1946 they had 46
and 43 MPs) and even the Social Democrats came out
of this election greatly reduced (1946 - 37 MPs).
Only the Slovak Freedom Party increased its
representation from 3 to 4 MPs.

The Assembly, which met for the first time
on 10 June 1948, was despite its artificial
fixed representation still a parliament, for the
Communist Party was not yet sure how it would
rule Czechoslovakia.  Parliament still remained
the only gate to power.  All the government
ministers stood as deputies for the election and
were the first to swear allegiance to the Republic.
Politically it was still the most prestigious

body; moreover, the Assembly was bent on
continuing to organise its work in the traditional
fashion. It elected its praesidium and a
perplexing number of committees and commissions
to enable itself to exercise effectively its
legislative and controlling powers. (A. Novotny
was thus elected for the first time; A. Dubcek
followed in a bye-election.)

The Communist Party had elected to it its
most capable members and party leaders were
members of the government. The praesidium
elected on the first day was headed by a minority
(Social Democratic) leader, Dr O. John, and while
it had a Communist majority, all the other parties,
except the Slovak Freedom Party, had several
members on it. This body was still only
responsible for managing plenary sessions and
preparing agendas. It retained a relatively
large secretariat of civil servants who not only
secured the administration of the praesidium
business, but also of the Assembly and its
committees and sub-committees. While committee
and sessional minutes were supervised by members
of parliament (and approved by the Assembly) the
secretariat kept detailed records of sessions,
committee meetings and voting. Curiously this
secretariat survived almost intact all the
ensuing changes that the National Assembly was
subject to.


Election in 1954

After Gottwald's death (and the end of the cult
of personality) the party decided that
parliamentary elections as well as elections to
all the types of national councils (local
government) should be held. Since 1948, when
the last election had taken place, the country,
parliamentary and electoral laws had been
transformed, to such a degree that it was
unthinkable that as many as 10-20 percent of the
electorate should somehow express their
disagreement with the regime as happened in the

1948 election. Parliament was now completely modelled on the Supreme Soviet, hence the accepted electoral results of over 99 per cent for that body would have to occur in Czechoslovakia.

Shortly before its dissolution parliament passed new electoral laws. According to Act 26/1954, members of parliament were to be elected in single constituencies of 35,000 electors. Candidates were still selected from the composite lists put forward by the National Front (in which the Communist Party had a preponderant majority), but instead of voting for party lists of the National Front as in 1948, electors were asked to vote for individual candidates. If elected (and since no opposition candidates, unapproved by the National Front, were allowed to stand, this was a foregone conclusion) individual members would be responsible directly to their electors, which was acclaimed as a democratic advance on the system in force in 1948. In fact the arrangement was introduced in order to produce the near hundred per cent results comparable to the Soviet Supreme Soviet.

In Czechoslovak conditions in 1954, the election was all the same a trial of efficiency for the Communist Party, and it was something quite unprecedented. The country was divided into new administrative units in 1949 only, and constituencies had to conform to these new units. The new party structures would be put to a test and however controlled, elections in Czechoslovakia were always a risky enterprise. The central National Front's task was easy: it fixed the proportional representation of the Communist Party and other parties. But the constituency National Fronts had to select candidates themselves, and have them subsequently approved by the higher echelon of the National Front.

There was a trial run for the new system in May 1954 when elections for local, district and regional councils took place. Despite tremendous organisational efforts by the Communist Party, between 5.4 and 6 per cent of the voters

85

## Table 3.5

### Parliamentary Preasidium
### (elected 10 June 1948)

Speaker:     Dr O. John (Social Democrat)

Deputies:
- V. David (KSC)
- B. Hodinova-Spurna (KSC)
- F. Komzala (KSS)
- J. Mjartan (SSO)
- Dr D. Polansky (CSL)
- Dr V. Prochazka (KSC)
- F. Richler (CSS)
- J. Valo (KSS)

Members:
- K. Bacilek (KSS)
- G. Bares (KSC)
- D. Bartuska (KSC)
- M. Culen (KSS)
- J. Franek (KSC)
- Z. Hejzlar (KSC)
- J. Jura (KSC)
- Dr J. Kokes (KSC)
- F. Koktan (CSS)
- Dr Mouralova (KSS)
- J. Smrkovsky (KSC)
- J. Steka (KSC)
- F. Tymes (Social Democrat)
- S. Vojanec (CSL)

Abbreviations:
- KSC : Communist Party of Czechoslovakia
- KSS : Communist Party of Slovakia
- CSS : Czech Socialist Party
- CSL : Czech People's (Catholic) Party
- SSO : Slovak Reival Party
- SSS : Slovak Freedom Party

Social Democrats were fused in June 1948 and henceforth were members of the Communist Party

actually voted against the National Front candidates, while only a marginal number, 0.4 per cent, spoilt their ballot papers to express their disapproval of the regime. However, this opposition found no expression in the representation in the councils, and as a result measures were taken to improve electoral performance in the future. It was decided that in the parliamentary election in November 1954, elecors would cast their votes publicly and in a corporate manner. In fact people were marched out of factories, farms and offices to ballot places and voted for National Front candidates directly without any recourse to the screen which was there to ensure secrecy.

But even then results proved disappointing. While the percentage of the (blank) opposition vote was halved - (only 2.11 per cent voted against the National Front in the parliamentary election, and only 2.73 per cent voted against official Slovak candidates in the election for the Slovak National Council which took place simultaneously) - it became obvious that the Communist Party had not yet mastered election techniques and could not produce results comparable to those of the Supreme Soviet, or other East European parliaments. In addition, the party was dissatisfied with the composition of the National Assembly, for too many local politicians, unknown to the central committee apparat in Prague, succeeded in getting themselves elected. In 1957 another round of local government elections took place and the organisation of this election was so vastly improved that only 1.1 per cent voted against the National Front in the Czech provinces, while in Slovakia only 0.55 per cent dared to vote against the official candidates.


Election in 1960

In 1960 the country was once again administratively reorganised and was given a new constitution which proclaimed Czechoslovakia a socialist republic, thus making it ideologically equal of the USSR. Since the number of regions and districts had been reduced, constituencies had to be redrawn. Instead of constituencies with a fixed number of voters it was decided to fix the number of members of parliament (300 instead of the previous 315). Once again the National Front put forward its candidates, and after the perfective measures employed in 1957 had been applied, the results finally showed that the Communist Party had the system firmly under its control. All the electoral results exceeded 99 per cent; still regions with opposition in the past returned the lowest results: Central Slovakia 99.5 per cent, Eastern Slovakia 99.73 per cent, Northern Slovakia 99.76 per cent, and South Moravia 99.88 per cent. Council elections which took place simultaneously with the parliamentary ones proved even more satisfactory: regional councils polled 99.88 per cent; district 99.82 per cent, local 99.76 per cent.

It is probable that this election was very closely controlled because the Communist Party intended to revive the National Assembly and give greater powers to the councils. Once again the Speaker, Z. Fierlinger, was member of the politburo of the Communist Party, and his primary task was to keep the Assembly under close control. The central National Front not only fixed the proportionate representation of classes and groups, but also carefully picked candidates. All the important party office holders became candidates in this election: they came to represent the working class, instead of the unknown workers from industry as was the case in 1954. Despite meticulous care, twelve local candidates failed to be elected in the parallel council election, which clearly indicated that the weakest point of the control system was on the local level.


Election in 1964

This was the most successfully organised election

since 1948. Not only did all the regions return 99.90 per cent of votes and over, but also in the parallel election to local government councils, only five candidates out of the overall number of 228,587 failed to be elected. In fact the election was so successfully managed that it inspired the Communist Party to think of experiments for the next one due in 1968. Up to 1964 the preparation of the election consisted of three phases: (1) the National Front committees selected candidates for each seat; (2) registered them (or had them approved by the central party); and (3) presented them to the electors at public meetings. It was now projected that at stage one, National Front committees should select several candidates for each seat, and ask public meetings of electors to approve one of the proposed. It was even envisaged to have two candidates in some constituencies in the final phase, so that voters would have at least in some cases a choice between two National Front candidates.

However, the election of 1968 did not take place and was postponed until 1971. During that eventful year the National Assembly was working on several projects of electoral laws, but they were not passed. Only after the 1969-71 period of purges did the Federal Assembly pass new electoral laws. They, however, appear to be the pre-1968 ones; the same three procedural stages and single candidates in each constituency. The only innovation is that voters vote simultaneously for all the legislative and local bodies: the Federal Parliament (the Peoples and Nations Chambers), Czech and Slovak National Councils and regional, district and local councils. Another innovation was that for the first time a 'socialist opposition' group (purged Communists) campaigned with leaflets and unofficial appeals against candidates of the National Front.

Election Results 1964

| | Registered Voters | Participated | National Front | Percentage |
|---|---|---|---|---|
| Czechoslovakia | 9,487,298 | 9,432,147 | 9,412,309 | 99.84 |
| Czech Provinces | | | | 99.93 |
| Slovakia | | | | 99.94 |

Election in 1971

This was the first election under the federal
arrangements and was chiefly important from the
external point of view: its results went to prove
how far the country had been 'normalised'. Quite
contrary to the past precedents, the chairman of
the central electoral committee became the
secretary of the Communist Party, A. Indra. He
was the chief organiser of the election and was
primarily responsible for the results. Another
unprecedented occurence: the election was held in
two days, on Friday and Saturday, 29 and 30
November 1971. As usual voters were asked to
vote publicly, i.e. put the National Front ballot
papers directly into the ballot box without going
behind a screen which was placed at the back of
the election room. However, the results justified
the immense effort that the Communist Party put
into organising the election: A. Indra resigned
as secretary of the central committee and was
rewarded with the post of the Federal Speaker, thus
becoming the second most powerful person in the
Czechoslovak political system (see Table 3.6).

Electoral Campaigns

Traditionally elections in Czechoslovakia have
always been preceded by vigorous election campaigns.
Though after 1948 the Communist Party curtailed
the campaigns nonetheless, they have always been

Table 3.6

| | Registered Voters | Participation | % | N.F.SL | % | N.F.SN | % |
|---|---|---|---|---|---|---|---|
| Czechoslovakia | 10,253,796 | 10,197,234 | 99.45 | 10,153,572 | 99.81 | 10,144,464 | 99.77 |
| Czech Repbulic | 7.250,848 | 7,207,961 | 99.41 | 7,171,935 | 99.76 | 7,170,898 | 99.71 |
| Slovak Republic | 3,002,948 | 2,989,273 | 99.54 | 2,981,637 | 99.94 | 2,973,575 | 99.91 |

SL = Peoples Chamber of the Federal Assembly
SN = Nationality Chamber of the Federal Assembly

permitted and had a unique character. It is obvious from the discussion of the electoral laws in force in Czechoslovakia that quite a number of features of the pre-1948 system have been retained. The latest electoral campaign in November 1971, in spite of several new institutions, was on the whole typical. The election date was fixed two months in advance so that an electoral campaign could be 'prepared and conducted'. The praesidia of the Federal Assembly and the Czech and Slovak Councils made the election date known on 24 September 1971: it was fixed for 26 and 27 November 1971. Immediately three types of electoral committees were set up: (1) electoral committees of the National Front at all levels (central, regional, district, and local), whose task was to compile the lists of candidates; (2) electoral district committees organised by the Czech and Slovak National Councils; these committees organised electoral procedures and issued ballot papers; and (3) electoral district committees which supervised the ballot itself, provided buildings and rooms for the vote, counted the votes, and passed on the results to the central election commission. (There were 18,874 of these committees, with some 130,000 people involved, in the 1971 election.)

The election manifesto for 1971 was based on the resolutions and directives of the Fourteenth congress of the Communist Party of Czechoslovakia which took place in May 1971. All the branches of the National Front took this manifesto as the basis for their electoral statements. The manifesto was presented to the electorate together with the candidates. Electoral meetings took place during the first month of the electoral campaign. There are no national figures of these meetings but the North Moravian Region published its own: between 5 and 30 September 1971 the regional Communist Party organised meetings attended by 302,650 citizens; some 30,000 questions were asked by the participants. At these meetings people could not only object to the election manifesto (no one actually did!) but also to the candidates. No modifications to the manifesto were suggested and all the candidates were approved: consequently they were officially registered by the district committees and their names printed on the ballot papers.

In the next phase agitation centres were set up all over Czechoslovakia: some 7,867 in 1971 as contrasted by some 5,000 in 1964. These agitation centres printed election manifestos and other literature and distributed them among the population. They also organised agitators duets (dvojice), election agents in twos, whose task was to visit every household in the country and ask for its support in the election. This task was fulfilled on 22-24 October 1971 when practically every citizen in Czechoslovakia was visited by these "duets". The rest of the campaign consisted of election meetings addressed by registered National Front candidates who attempted to convince electors that they were the right persons to represent them and carry out election promises contained in the manifesto.

For the ballot itself each elector was issued with an election card. On arriving at the election room he was checked against the electoral list and then given the ballot paper. The paper (or rather papers, for each elector voted simultaneously in the local, regional and national election) contained the name of the registered candidate: voters voted for the candidate by placing the ballot paper in the ballot box. To vote against the candidate the elector had to cross off the name of the candidate. This presumably required him to retire behind a screen where he could effect the modification. But this seemed dangerous. Electoral commissions could duly take note of such an elector, for all the citizens were asked by the National Front to vote publicly for its candidates: 99.81 per cent preferred to vote this way.

Even from this incomplete analysis of the campaign it is obvious that every election in Czechoslovakia is a great organisational feat. In 1971 for the first time all candidates were

elected to all the appropriate council, parliamentary or local government bodies.  The Communist
Party proved that it could undertake any political
task and ensure the greatest possible success.   In
this way it could consult the people without
necessarily giving them the widest possible
choice.


Committee System

The system of parliamentary committees and
commissions (these are ad hoc bodies while the
former are permanent) is the traditional way in
which the Czechoslovak National Assembly has always
set about its business.   Even after the
simplications following World War II, the
Constitutional Assembly (1946-48) abounded in
Committees and sub-committees.  The most important
committee in this parliament was the constitutional one (Act 197/17 October 1946) which
consisted of thirty-six members and was to achieve
the principal task of this Assembly, drafting a
new constitution.   Between 1946 and 1948 this
committee held twenty meetings and finally
presented the draft of the constitution to the
newly-elected Assembly in May 1948.

        Apart from this chief committee some
twenty-two other committees and commissions
functioned in the period of the Constitutional
Assembly.   The Verification Committee (held five
meetings) confirmed the validity of members'
election;   the Permanent Committee (one meeting)
looked after the business of parliament as such;
the Incompatibility Committee (one meeting) looked
into the business interest of members and made
sure that they were not contrary to the
constitutional laws.   However, these were on the
whole quiet bodies;   other committees were kept
fairly busy.   Thus the Foreign Affairs Committee
(twenty-four members) held twenty-three meetings,
the Agricultural Committee (thirty members) held
seventy-four meetings, while the Trade and Commerce
Committee held thirty-nine meetings.   The

Immunity Committee (eighteen members), which was entitled to lift parliamentary immunity from members, met nineteen times, while the Cultural Committee (twenty-four members) met twenty-five times. The Army Committee (24 members) was kept rather busy at twenty-nine meetings, while the Security Committee was even busier with thirty-one meetings during which matters of national security were discussed and decided upon. It can be said that every member of parliament sat on at least one committee; committees met in the intervals between plenary sessions and the latter were quite frequent. A member of parliament was kept fully occupied and members certainly earned their parliamentary salaries.

It seems obvious that even after the coup d'état in February 1948 and the 'restricted' election in May 1948, the Communist Party could think of no better way than to continue parliamentary activity on practically the same basis as before. At the first plenary session of the new Assembly committees were elected. Though their number was slightly reduced they still covered all the important aspects of national life and it was obvious that they would not only discuss and formulate policies as well as prepare legislation, but also exercise control in their respective fields. The separate committees, Army and Security, were united and brought under the control of the secretary general of the Communist Party, R. Slansky, who became chairman. Another important committee, Agriculture, was chaired by another influential Communist leader, J. Smrkovsky. The Foreign Affairs Committee came under V. Novy, Legal and Constitutional under Dr Bartuska, Cultural under Koubek. Budgetary under Valo, Economic under Mrs Mouralova, and Trade and Commerce under Horn. The Communist Party, as the strongest in this parliament, took over decisive control of all the vital committees: only several unimportant ones (the corresponding ministries were controlled by the same party) were left to members of other parties. Thus the Social Democrats chaired the Food Committee (Mrs Jungwirthova) and Control and Savings Committee

(Lindauer) while the Socialists chaired the Social Security and Health Committee (Matl). Christian Democrats chaired the Incompatibility Committee (Dr Batek) and Control of the Two Year Plan Committee (Dr Berak). The Slovak Democrats, now renamed as the Slovak Revival Party, chaired only one committee, the Initiative Committee (Dr Stefanik) which clearly indicated that very little initiative would be left to this committee.

It appears that in the initial period of this parliament, most of these committees were kept very busy because between June 1948 and October 1949 the Assembly passed a record number of laws which transformed Czechoslovakia into a Communist state and the Assembly itself into a body resembling the Supreme Soviet. Unfortunately no analysis of committee meetings is available; by then committee proceedings had become state secrets and were no longer published. In this parliament there was an additional reason for frequent committee meetings. According to the new constitution, members of the Assembly were no longer full-time paid members; they retained their previous jobs and were only paid for the missed working hours of their employment. However, the Speaker and the praesidium members were still full-time and were paid full parliamentary salaries. Members of committees were paid special allowances for attending committee meetings and since the important committees met very frequently they were still full-time paid parliamentarians.

It is not clear when wholesale simplifications of the committee system did occur. In June 1948 some sixteen committees were formed and members elected to them. In October 1949, when new procedural rules were introduced into the Assembly, the system of committees was probably also modified. Six committees disappeared altogether and the remaining ten were substantially reorganised to cover additional fields. The Army and Security Committee continued to exist (thirty members) under R. Slansky's chairmanship, but it disappeared soon afterwards, together with its chairman, who was tried and executed for high treason. The Foreign Affairs Committee only changed its chairman: Dr V. Prochazka was substituted for V. Novy, who had been arrested and remained in prison for some time. Other committees retained their initial chairmen: the Economic Committee (Mrs Mouralova), the Cultural Committee (L. Koubek), the Agricultural Committee (J. Smrkovsky, soon to be arrested and imprisoned), the Budgetary Committee (J. Valo), the Social Security and Health Committee (J. Matl), the Constitutional and Legal Committee (Dr J. Bartuska). The Immunity Committee was transformed into the Mandate Committee and Dr L. Kokes remained its chairman, though he probably had precious little to do with the immunity of members: the most vigorous purge of the Assembly was launched at this stage. The Control of the Two Year Plan Committee was transformed into the Committee of Economic Planning and Control and remained under the Christian Democratic chairman, Professor Dr J. Berak. These changes indicated that parliamentary committees lost almost entirely their former powers of control; they also ceased to discuss policies and bills. Draft bills must be presented directly to the Assembly at its plenary meetings which took place at monthly intervals. Bills were passed almost without discussion.

After the election in 1954 which took place at the end of the personality cult period, everyone hoped, above all the members, for a revival of parliament and hence of its committees. But these expectations were not fulfilled. Although the new Speaker became Z. Fierlinger, an old parliamentarian (member of the Communist Party praesidium), and even the first secretary and praesidium member, A. Novotny, was elected to the parliamentary praesidium, instead of revival the process of simplifcation was continued; above all, the work of the Assembly and the committees themselves was still further paralysed by the affluence of new, inexperienced members. In 1954 only seven committees were formed and even their membership was restricted (in 1957 practically all

of them doubled their memberships). The Mandate
Committee with eleven members was chaired by
J. Vodicka, originally a practising butcher.  The
Cultural Committee, now intended to supervise
'cultural industries', had nineteen members and
was presided over by Jan Drda, the 'official'
writer.  The Economic and Budget Commitee with
twenty-seven members was chaired by J. Stetka, a
glass worker, while the Agricultural Committee
(thirty-four members) was run by V. Krutina,
professional party organiser, soon to become
Minister of Agriculture.  Only the committees
chaired by non-party members were composed of
suitably qualified deputies but as a consequence
were of little political significance.  Professor
Dr J. Berak (Christian Democrat) chaired the
Foreign Affairs Committee, while Professor Dr
K. Kacl (Liberal Socialist) chaired the Health
Committee.  Another expert lawyer, Dr J. Krofta,
chaired the Constitutional and Legal Committee
which, however, had very little to do.

Only in 1957 did the Communist Party begin
to think of really reviving the Assembly.  To
start with, parliamentary committes doubled their
membership, so that a reasonable proportion of
members would take part in parliamentary work.
In 1960 the party's wish for revival and better
use of the committees became public knowledge, but
on the whole this had little effect on the
National Assembly after the election in 1960.
Only one new committee (for Industry) was formed
and other committees were strengthened by having
as their chairmen  important party leaders.
J. Harus chaired the Mandate Committee, I. Skala
the Cultural Committee, J. Valo the Plan and
Budget Committee, J. Boruvka the Agricultural
Committee, V. Skoda the Constitutional and Legal
Committee, H. Leflerova the Foreign Affairs
Committee, while the new Committee for Industry
was chaired by an expert, A. Bichler.  The Health
Committee only was controlled by the non-
Communist Slovak, A. Ziak, while the rest were
presided over by Communist leaders who were at
least members of the party's central committee.
It was during this period, 1960-64, that the

Communist Party allowed public debates on the role
of parliament and finally decided on strengthening
its powers and prestige.   The party also invited
non-Communists to present their own proposals and
a comprehensive package was subsequently approved
at the Twelfth congress of the Communist Party in
1962.   The effects of this 'package' were to be
felt after the election in 1964.

At the first plenary session after the
election, on 12 June 1964, the new Assembly formed
eleven committees:   the Mandate Committee
(twelve members) was chaired by the Christian
Democratic member, M. Pospisil, while the Committee
for Trade, Service, Communications and Consumer
Industries (twenty-eight members) was chaired by
a Liberal, L. Dohnal.   The Health Committee
(twenty-six members) was presided over  by a non-
party professional, Dr A. Petrusova.   The rest
of them were chaired by important party members,
some of whom were going to play an important part
in the liberalisation of the system in 1968.
Dr V. Skoda, former Minister of Justice, and a
rigid central committee member, controlled the
Committee for  Legal and Constitutional matters,
while another, Mrs Leflerova, presided over the
Committee for Local Councils.   The Foreign Affairs
Committee was under the control of the 'liberal'
central committee member, Dr F. Kriegel, while
another 'liberal' Communist, A. Polednak, chaired
most liberally the Committee for Culture.   An
experienced deputy, and former Social Democratic
deputy, F. Tymes, chaired the Committee for Plan
and Budget, while, A. Bichler retained the
chairmanship of the Committee for Industry and
Transport.   The Slovak Communist, G. Gabruska,
controlled the Committee for Investments and
Building, and V. Kucera chaired the Committee for
Agriculture and Food.   Often the vice-chairmen
of the committees headed by Communist members were
non-Communists, and non-Communist representation
on the committees was striking.   The membership
of the committees was increased;  they averaged
twenty-five members, thus giving every member of
this parliament a chance to perform parliamentary
duties on at least one of them.   Committees

encompassed almost the whole of the national life, except the army and the security, which still remained under the exclusive control of the Communist Party's central committee, the so-called Eighth Department.

In April 1968 changes began to be felt even in this 'liberal' National Assembly. Though the Novotnyite deputies refused to resign, the Speaker, B. Lastovicka, and the praesidium did stand down. J. Smrkovsky, the reformer, was elected Speaker and the newly elected praesidium also wanted reforms and changes. It became the task of the committees to prepare these changes; the frequency of their meetings more than doubled and in June and December 1968 they met every day, almost without interruption. Only one new committee was created, for Army and Security, and was chaired by an experienced Communist, L. Hofman. Another committee, Peoples Control, was taken away from the government's jurisdiction and became a parliamentary committee. But otherwise no great changes were made in the structure and procedures of the committees, though judging from the large number of committees of the newly established Czech and Slovak National Councils new committees were also envisaged for the National Assembly which became the Federal Assembly on 1 January 1969.

The election for the new federal system did not take place in 1968 and was delayed until November 1971, when the Communist Party considered the country sufficiently 'normalised'. After the election, when the newly elected Federal Assembly and the councils formed their committees, it became clear that the new regime would continue the 1964-8 practice of allowing all the legislative assemblies to work through their committees. In the Federal Assembly, each chamber formed eight committees, which included the Army and Security one. Completely new people were elected to preside over the committees, and only two of them were members of the party's central committee: Dr Pennigerova, the Social Security Committee (Peoples Chamber) and Dr Auersperg, the Foreign

Affairs Committee (Nations Chamber). Dr Nejezchleb, a complete newcomer (formerly chairman of the Sports Association) was elected chairman of the Army and Security Committee and his counterpart in the Nations Chamber became Dr Mandak, member of the party's Central Control Commission. Both National Councils elected nine committees each. In the Czech Council two committees were put under non-Communist chairman (Committee for Trade and Transport: F. Toman, Christian Democrat; Health and Security Committee: V. Jedlicka, Liberal-Socialist). The rest were chaired by party leaders, none of whom, however, reached central committee status. The Slovak National Council elected nine chairmen, all of whom were Communist Party members; non-Communist leaders (J. Gajdosik and Dr M. Zakovic) were elected as Deputy Speakers of the Council.


Laws and Legislative Processes

Legislative processes in Czechoslovakia are rooted in ancient historical traditions and are in many ways unique. Because of the party system, individual deputies have always been less important than parliamentary party clubs. Thus questions (interpellations) in the Assembly have never been asked by individuals, nor did individuals advance bills (private member's bills do not exist): it has always been a party group which either asked questions or initiated legislation.

Legislative initiative often did not even originate from the parliamentary party but from the political party as such. To demonstrate this unique Czechoslovak way of legislating, let us consider the following example: in 1934 the Social Democratic Party wanted a new social insurance act covering all the working population in Czechoslovakia. Ideas for such a law were first voiced at a party conference and then discussed by the party praesidium. The party praesidium then engaged in talks with other parties, especially the members of the ruling coalition.

Afterwards the party put its proposals to the
Minister of National Insurance, who was also a
member of the Social Democratic Party.  The
minister asked civil servants to prepare a bill
which he subsequently presented to parliament.
The relevant parliamentary committee discussed
the bill, amended it and returned it to the
ministry for amendment.  After it had passed
through this stage, the Speaker presented the
bill to a plenary session which then passed it and
it became a law.  Once passed by the Assembly,
a bill becomes a law after it has been signed by
the President and published in the statute book
of Acts (Sbirka zakonu).  It is a long and
sometimes cumbersome way of passing laws, but it
seems to have worked well between 1918 and 1939
and again from 1945 to 1948 so as to satisfy the
citizens of Czechoslovakia.  After the Communist
coup d'état in 1948, the Communist Party hardly
altered the process:  the initiative stage was
slightly simplified, but otherwise all remained
unchanged.  The party, or its central committee,
discusses ideas for a new law;  the party
praesidium then instructs the relevant ministry
to prepare a bill which is presented to the
parliamentary committee  to be discussed,
amended and possibly returned to the ministry for
redrafting.  When finally the bill is passed by
the Assembly plenary session (with or without
division - unanimously) it is promulgated in the
customary constitutional way.  In addition to
this simplification (the party takes the initiative
throughout) the Communist Party introduced two
other modifications:  in 1962 it established
party commissions which generated ideas for new
legislation;  and the relevant departments of the
Communist Party prepare  these ideas in the form
of proposals for the praesidium and the ministry.

     It should be stressed that since the
establishment of the Communist regime in February
1948 the Assembly had been extremely busy with
discussing and passing laws.  While it is
impossible to gauge the activity of the Assembly
and its committees (committee proceedings are state
secrets and are not published, a pre-war regulation)

it is clear from the number of laws passed that
the Communist Party wanted to use the Assembly to
accomplish all its political plan.  Perhaps a
little paradoxically, the busiest parliament
proved to be the one elected in 1948.   This
Assembly counted among its achievements the
dissolution of the pre-1948 system, its own
dissolution into a Supreme Soviet, as well as
passing the greatest number of laws ever, over
332 Acts.   Some of these laws were unimportant
(Act 32 dealt with the establishment and finance
of theatres;  Act 43 agricultural credits, etc.),
but most of them were of a fundamental nature.
Thus Act 46 dealt with agricultural reforms which
had far-reaching effects, while Act 114 meant
further nationalisation and had a tremendous impact
on the further development of industry.   Act 118
nationalised wholesale trade and Act 120 all
businesses with more than fifty employees.
Acts 181, 183, 187 and 199 reorganised the money
market, investment banks, co-operatives and
communal enterprises.   Act 280 reorganised the
country administratively, replacing the historical
land division with regions, while Act 286
reorganised the police and security.   The
security of the new system was embodied in Act 231
which introduced quite a number of new crimes
against the state and increased penalties for
them.   Act 247 established labour camps in which
those convicted under the previous Act could serve
their sentences.   Act 319 reorganised the
judiciary:  in the term of this Act any citizen
could be appointed judge by the Ministry of
Justice.   Act 322 reorganised barristers and
solicitors, destroyed their independence and made
them employees of a state organisation.   Many Acts
regulated the economy, foreign trade and even
artists' titles and it is obvious that at least
the parliamentary committees must have sat almost
continuously.

        It is true that in 1949 this feverish
activity abated a little, but all the same some
280 Acts were passed by the Assembly, several of
them of the most fundamental nature.   Act 60 was
the most important one:  it dealt with economic

planning in Czechoslovakia. Several Acts (76, 87, 139) dealt with the administration of the capital, of local and district units, while Act 269 reorganised national insurance. In addition agricultural collectives were given a legal basis and research and documentation was centrally organised (Act 261). In 1949 the Assembly also passed revised procedures and these for a long time put an end to 'excessive' legislation (they were revised again in 1954). The new procedures not only simplified the passing of Acts by the Assembly - its praesidium was given increased legislative powers - but also limited plenary sessions and debates.

It is not surprising that in 1950 'only' some 191 Acts were passed and none of these was extremely important. Act 31 changed the statute of the Czechoslovak State Bank, Act 150 similarly treated the Czechoslovak Post Office. Doctors were newly organised (Act 197), insurance reorganised (Act 190) and peace was taken out of controversy, elevated to a law and any war propaganda made punishable by law (Act 165). In 1951 when only some 128 Acts were passed, the legislators concentrated on tying up the loose ends of legislation passed in the two previous years. The nationalised building industry was reorganised (Act 58) as well as nationalised shops and trading enterprises (Act 64). Act 68 regulated the status of voluntary organisations and gatherings. The Ministry of State Control was established (Act 73) as well as other ministries and Slovak ministries (poverenictva) (Acts 74, 75). Universities were reorganised (Act 80), state farms were established (Act 82) as well as tractor stations (Act 83). New laws were passed governing the professions of barristers, solicitors and notaries (Acts 114, 115, 116). Act 69 reorganised the protection of state borders which until then did not require any special legislation. In 1952 the legislators concentrated on such important activities as fishing (Act 62), sea shipping (Act 61), on the establishment of the Academy of Sciences (Act 52) and Academy of Agricultural Sciences (Act 90), and this seems to have exhausted them for that year.

However, three Acts passed in the year 1952 were of fundamental importance: Act 64 once again reorganised and put on a new basis the courts and the procuracy, while Acts 65 and 66 dealt specifically with the structures of courts and the procuracy. Although the number of Acts passed by the Assembly in 1953 (some 115) surpassed that of 1952, they were all without exception quite unimportant. Act 31 dealt with primary education and teachers training, Act 79 was really a supplement to a law governing the title of national artists, Act 81 put the local government (Communist self-governing councils) under the direction of the central government, while Act 115 regulated authors' rights. In 1954 the Assembly passed several laws modifying electoral laws governing elections to the Assembly, the Slovak National Council as well as local councils (Acts 12, 13, 26, 27) and quickly passed into history, leaving behind a jungle of 'laws' and an utterly 'exhausted' (purged) Assembly.

In 1954 the new Assembly started auspiciously with a new set of procedural rules. It was hoped that by re-emphasising committee work the Assembly would revive and possibly become the political instrument it once was in 1948 (Acts 61, 62). These re-establishment efforts, however, seem to have exhausted the legislative body and all the repressive 'laws' of the period of personality cult remained in force, unamended. The 1954 Assembly soon proved that even when committees were revived the Assembly as a body was not. Plenary sessions were rarely convoked and the praesidium still held the control and balance in its own hands. The Assembly passed some fifty-one Acts in 1955; none of which proved very significant. They ranged from the usual Plan for 1955 (Act 12) to the establishment and dissolution of research institutes (Act 14), the statutes of spas (Act 43), and of nationalised enterprises (Act 51). However, in the same year, the praesidium itself passed some sixty-four

'legal measures' which all had the force of law:
legal measure 21 established the praesidium of
the Supreme Court; 22 established wood inspection;
23 dealt with poisons;  58 covered children's
allowances, 59 regulated salary rate of judges,
procurators and probationary lawyers;  61 amended
the divorce law;  64 amended the Health Act 103
(1951) and medical care therein.

Even though in 1956 the Assembly passed
more laws (some sixty-nine) than the praesidium
'legal measures' (some sixty-one) the praesidium
still dominated legislative activity and it
became obvious that this Assembly would not
recover from the blows dealt to it by the
personality cult.   However, the Acts passed in
1956 indicate that this year started a process
of recovery.   Act 33 once again tackled Slovak
administration and strengthened its autonomy.
Act 40 dealt with the protection of nature, 45
shortened the labour week, 46 amended the law on
universities, 47 dealt with civil aviation, while
in Act 55 social security was tackled again.
However, more important Acts came later in that
year, possibly as a result of the Twentieth
Communist Party congress in the USSR.   Act 63
revised the criminal justice law of 1950;
Act 64 amended criminal procedures, Act 65
reorganised courts;  and Act 69 revised the tax
system.   These were all important and
fundamental Acts, while the praesidium 'legal
measures' dealt with limited but concrete problems
(e.g. Numbers 30 and 31 regulated teachers' and
doctors' salaries respectively).

In 1957 'reform' Acts continued to be
passed (some eighty-two).   Act 10 amended the
Act dealing with national committees (local
government and local administration);   Act 14
amended the criminal administrative law (88-1950)
while Act 24 covered thieving and pilfering of
nationalised property.   Act 26 fixed notaries
charges, Act 32 covered national health care of
armed forces, and Act 35 dealt with technical
co-ordination.   Act 34 regulated the election
of peoples and professional judges, while Act 37

defined their powers and responsibilities.  Act
53 amended the statute of the Academy of Science,
while Act 70 established the Institute of
Social Sciences attached to the central
committee of the Communist Party.  Act 75
regulated identity cards and Act 76 amended
the residential regulations of Czechoslovak
citizens and foreigners.

In 1958 the Assembly passed some eighty-
nine Acts while 'legal measures' amounted only to
some thirty-two.  Act 16 amended the statute
of the Czechoslovak Red Cross, Act 41 social
security, Act 43 the State Bank and Act 64
currency regulations.  Act 40 regulated the
incomes of imprisoned citizens and Act 69
regulated the inter-relations of Communist
countries.  Two important economic Acts were
passed in this year, both regulating planning in
nationalised industries and territorial
planning.  Last but not least Act 87 systematised
housing and building regulations.  The year
1958, however, is interesting from another
point of view.  While previously the information
media gave publicity to only the most important
plenary sessions of the Assembly, henceforth
they pay systematic attention to this body and
its activity.  Between 1948-54 the National
Assembly held some 85 plenary meetings;  hardly
any had been reported in the communication media.
Between 1954-60 some thirty-eight plenary meetings
had taken place and since 1958 they commanded
the attention of the press at least.  Of the
eight plenary meetings which took place in 1958,
five were reported in the press (Rude pravo of
24 January, 4 July, 17 October and 13 December
1958).  During 1959 this attention increased
still further:  of the eight plenary meetings of
that year, six were extensively covered in
addition to one praesidium meeting (the praesidium
held six meetings) and one committee meeting
(foreign affairs).  In 1960 there were only
three plenary meetings and all three were reported
in the press together with a praesidium appeal to
the Soviet Supreme Soviet of the USSR on the
international situation and disarmament.

Between 1960-64 the Assembly passed through
a phase of substantial recovery, though it
'recovered' fully only after 1964. The
praesidium still animated and held some fifty-
seven meetings while plenary sessions amounted to
twenty-six, which was an average of six sessions
a year. Throughout this Assembly plenary
sessions were reported, sometimes in great detail.
In April 1961 Rude pravo reported not only the
jubilant debates of the successes of the FYP but
also the newly-passed law on the defence of
Czechoslovakia and on the establishment of peoples
courts (RP 18 and 19 April 1961). In June 1961
detailed accounts of the session reported the
adoption of new laws: they dealt with the Central
Office of State Control and Statistics, national
committees (further amendments), public order,
protection of health and the new organisation of
courts (RP 27 and 28 June 1961). In September
1961 the Prosecutor General's report to the
Assembly on socialist legality was given publicity
(20 September 1961), while a month later the new
penal code was publicised as well as routine
economy debates dealt with (RP 20 Nobember 1961).
By contrast the year 1962 meant a relative decrease
of interest in the Assembly. Only two plenary
meetings and debates were reported extensively
(RP 22 February and 30 March 1962), but two
committee meetings were given publicity. In 1963
all the meetings were given detailed publicity
(RP 25 January, 7 March, 10 July 26 September,
5 and 6 December 1963) as well as the three last
plenary meetings in 1964 (RP 31 January,
27 February and 5 June 1964). Throughout this
session the praesidium still dominated the
Assembly and plenary sessions tended to pass laws
in batches (for example, six laws were passed on
10 July 1963). This state of affairs continued
even after the Communist Party's congress late in
1962 at which decisions were made to increase the
powers and political role of the National Assembly.
The real implementation of this decision took
place after the general election on 2 June 1964.

On 24 and 25 June 1964 the first plenary
session of the Assembly elected a new praesidium,

approved the government programme and elected an increased number of committees. When in September 1964 the Second session took place, Mrs Leflerova announced new powers and improved conditions for the work of the National Assembly to the deputies as well as the country (RP 25 September 1964). Ministers who attended this session also promised improved performance: Krajcir promised a better plan, Dvorak better finance, and Neuman better justice. In October 1964 the foreign affairs committee's meeting was publicised and the two-day debate on the plan and the budget in December 1964 received detailed coverage (RP 10 and 12 December 1964). Though the Assembly was launched with a bang, there was no noticeable difference in its activity in 1965. Four plenary sessions took place in that year which passed several important laws: the Sixth plenary meeting passed a new labour code, social security legislation, while the Eighth session reorganised central administration, economy and improved the position of the Slovak National Council. More significantly, the Assembly refused to pass three bills: the one dealing with authors' fees, the others with vehicle tax and the amended criminal code. The bills went back to committees and thence to the government department for re-drafting. This was indeed something quite unprecedented and indicated that at long last the Assembly was taking itself seriously. It was a return to the ways and atmosphere immediately after the coup d'état, and even prior to it.

In 1966 the Assembly again held the prerequisite number of plenary sessions (four), but the debates were lively and once again proved unprecedented. The university bill, health bill and other bills were debated in the keenest fashion, which made it quite clear that the praesidium had lost itsfirm control on the debates, agenda and choice of speakers. Debates in the committees and plenary sessions resulted in amendments and even redrafting. Moreover, questions were asked by individual deputies thus reviving the old custom of interpellations: members asked numerous questions about the development of the capital, Prague, and shortcomings in the national economy. While the ministers concerned were under constitutional obligation to produce answers to these questions, they successfully evaded the responsibility. In 1967 the Assembly held four plenary meetings, at which debates continued to be lively, while in the committees, hard struggle with the government continued. The agriculture committee returned to the Ministry of Finance its bill on agricultural tax and collectives' contributions to the national health service. The Legal and Constitutional committees criticised a bill on the rights of assembly, for which prior application was necessary. The Police Act was passed by 115 to 87 votes only after an amendment on parliamentary immunity. But, as J. Smrkovsky, Speaker in 1968, put it, many laws were passed against the better judgement of the Assembly, in the name of party discipline.

Although in the short months of 1968 the National Assembly finally resumed all its historical powers, all the same the 'liberal' period 1964-8 bears a very favourable comparison with them. The secretary general of the Assembly office, Dr V. Kaigl, summarised most aptly this period:

"As a result of the Communist Party's decisions in 1964, the deformations in the relation between the party and parliament have been put right. Immediately the central committee ceased to issue detailed instructions to parliament and the neglected three hundred (deputies) began to perform their tasks in earnest. On the positive side the Assembly was responsible for the restructuring of industry, agriculture, house building and protection of environment. On the negative side it still accepted too many easy explanations from the executive, which tolerated no control in defence and security fields."

However, in 1968 these negative points were put right and many more with them.

Composition

Until February 1948 the political composition of the National Assembly was of paramount importance. Both in the 1945-6 Provisional and the 1946-8 Constitutive Assemblies, the Communist Party was in a minority or at best had a theoretical majority, provided the Social Democrats voted with it. At the election of 26 May 1946 the results were as follows:

| | | |
|---|---|---|
| Communist Party of Czechoslovakia | 93 | deputies |
| Communist Party of Slovakia | 21 | " |
| Czechoslovak Socialist Party | 55 | " |
| Czechoslovak Christian Party | 46 | " |
| Slovak Democratic Party | 43 | " |
| Czechoslovak Social Democratic Party | 37 | " |
| Slovak Labour Party | 2 | " |
| Slovak Freedom Party | 3 | " |
| Total : | 300 | |

After the Communist coup d'état in 1948, when 230 deputies voted for the new government and ipso facto for a new regime, the political composition of the Assembly became much less important. Quite arbitrarily the Communist Party fixed its majority in the National Front, and the 1948 election reflected for the first time the Communist victory in the coup and also its crushing superiority. In both provinces, Czech

111

and Slovak, the Communist Party majority was fixed
at 70 per cent.  The remaining 30 per cent of
seats were split among the non-Communists.  Thus,
while the Czech and Slovak Communists returned
215 deputies, the Socialists were left with 23
and the Christian Party and Social Democrats with
exactly the same number.  In Slovakia the
Democrats, now renamed the Revival Party, had
twelve deputies and the Freedom Party four.  In
June 1948 the Social Democratic Party was
amalgamated with the Communist Party and still
further increased the party's majority in the
Assembly.  In the period of the personality cult
1949-53, both the Communist Party and the non-
Communist parties were mercilessly purged and
while the purged Communists were replaced by party
members, the purged non-Communists often lost
their Assembly seats.  It seems obvious that in
the 1954 and 1960 elections, both highly
experimental, the political composition of the
Assembly was remarkably fluid, but without an
exception the non-Communist parties registered
further losses in representation, while a new
element, non-party citizens, registered great
increases.

     For the 1964 election for which we have
exhaustive analyses, the political composition of
the Assembly was as follows:

Communist Party of Czechoslovakia        157 deputies

Communist Party of Slovakia               65     "

Czechoslovak Socialist Party              20     "

Czechoslovak Christian Party              20     "

Slovak Revival Party                       6     "

Slovak Freedom Party                       4     "

Non-Party Deputies                        23     "


The non-Communist deputies amounted to only one-third

of the Assembly and while they were in the praesidium, and while they practically all acted as deputy speakers or chairmen of parliamentary committees, their strength in the Assembly was non-existent. Their important offices belonged to them as arbitrarily as the very political composition of the National Assembly.

After twenty years of continuous setbacks, the revival of the non-Communist parties in the short period of reform in 1968 seemed incredible. At one stage, after the Assembly voted the members of the new Czech National Council, the two Czech non-Communist parties, the Socialists and Christian Democrats, succeeded in getting some fifty deputies elected to this new legislative body of one hundred. While this 'dangerous' composition of the Czech National Council was quickly rectified (its membership was raised to 150 and has remained so since), the non-Communist parties increased their representation considerably, as compared to the 1964 election, nonetheless. Before the 1971 election (and after the purges 1969-71) the political composition of the Federal Assembly was as follows:

Communist Party of Czechoslovakia          282 deputies
(both chambers, the Peoples and
the Nations now 400)

Non-Communist Parties                       62      "

Non-Party Members                           36      "


Czech National Council:

Communist Party of Czechoslovakia          117

Non-Communist Parties                       38

Non-Party Members                           16

Slovak National Council:

| | |
|---|---|
| Slovak Communist Party | 95 |
| Non-Communist Parties | 17 |
| Non-Party Members | 16 |

It is obvious that had the reforms been carried out in 1968, the strength of the non-Communist representation would have increased quite considerably. In addition it was proposed to re-establish the Social Democratic Party and its representation was fixed quite highly, for even before its official establishment disillusioned Communists were trying to join its ranks. However, the new leadership of the Communist Party elected in March 1969, under Dr Husak, decided not only to stop the increase in representation of the non-Communists, but once again practically eliminate the non-Communist parties. As if to compensate, the representation of non-party citizens was considerably increased. While figures and analyses are not yet available, it appears that, for example, the Christian Democratic Party was reduced to total insignificance: only 3,068 members were elected to all the representative bodies (the Federal Assembly, Czech National Council, regional, district, and local councils) whose combined membership amounts to 140,925 deputies. This loss contrasts with the resounding success of non-party candidates whose representation in one of the regions (North Moravia) reached 41.9 per cent. If this proportion was matched in all eleven regions of the Czechoslovak Republic, the non-party deputies would nationally have a theoretical majority, or at least parity with the Communist Party.

With the decline in importance of the political composition of the National (now Federal) Assembly, its social composition became an important controlling factor for the Communist Party of Czechoslovakia. In the two Assemblies prior to 1948 the social composition was of no practical importance. Parties which claimed to

114

represent the various social classes and groups
sent into the Assembly deputies originating from
these groups.  However, it seemed difficult to
tag a social class label on many a member of the
Assembly.  The Communist leader, K. Gottwald, was
a skilled carpenter brought up in a family of
smallholder farmers.  However, his active life
was spent as politician and journalist, and thus
he embodied in himself the Czech and Slovak
dilemma:  he was of peasant origin, worker by
training and self-made intellectual.  In 1945
of the forty Czech Communist deputies, only ten
were 'clear' intellectuals, while the remaining
thirty were divided almost equally between farmers
(smallholders) and workers (chiefly trade
unionists).  Of the ten intellectuals three were
students (J. Kazimour, V. Koucky, V. Kopecky who
never completed his studies) while four classed
themselves as officials which title presupposed
some kind of education and also a middle class
descent (R. Slansky, J. Dolansky, V. David,
O. Sling and H. Zimakova-Zemanova);  one was a
doctor (R. Bures) another was a writer
(L. Civrny) and the last a teacher (J. Gerlichova-
Petruskova).  However, what was really important
at this stage was that all the Communist
deputies were experienced parliamentarians who
knew the business of the Czechoslovak parliament
well and could now make it work politically and
constitutionally.  The Provisional Assembly
elected in 1946 similarly reflected the population
structure of Czechoslovakia:  some forty-six
deputies could be classed as the intelligentsia
(professional people, writers, officials, etc.)
while the rest, some two hundred and fifty four,
were almost equally divided between workers,
farmers and tradesmen.

　　　Thus only after the coup d'état in 1948 did
the social composition of the Assembly seem to
become important.  The Communist Party insisted
that not only its own representation should consist
of workers from industry, but also that of the
non-Communist parties.  There was obviously a
strong ideological reason for having an absolute
majority of workers and farmers in an Assembly

which at this stage was still the principal political instrument with which the Communist Party
wanted to rule Czechoslovakia.  A power reason
for this composition was that the Communist Party
wanted to be absolutely sure of its control of
parliament, and such a composition seems to have
guaranteed it.  Even in 1954 when the party
decided to re-establish the Assembly in Czechoslovak political life it continued to insist that
the composition remained rigidly "working class":
some forty-seven members of the intelligentsia
only were allowed into this Assembly.  Whatever
the party's intention might have been, this
Assembly consisting of a majority of new deputies,
elected for the first time, and two hundred and
fifty three deputies entering the Assembly
directly from factories and collective farms
could not possibly hope to revive the pre-1948
institution.

No complete data are available for the 1954
and 1960 parliaments, but it can safely be assumed
that some 80 per cent of the deputies were
workers and farmers (collectivised) elected
straight from their factories and farms, who were
quite inexperienced in the ways of the Assembly,
its business, role and its working.  In 1962,
however, after the party's decisions to increase
the Assembly's powers and make it play a more
important role in political life, the changes in
the social composition became significant.  In
the 1964 election when these decisions were finally
applied, workers and farmers elected to the
Assembly amounted to fifty-six each;  twenty-nine
deputies represented technical intelligentsia and
thirty-seven other intellectuals.  The army and
security had ten deputies in this parliament, while
one hundred and one deputies were public servants
or professional politicians.  (In addition there
were ten deputies who were retired men and one
housewife.)  Although the largest group of
deputies (one hundred and one professional
politicians) consisted almost entirely of
politicians of working class origin, this group
now included a large number of former deputies
rehabilitated after the Twelfth congress in 1962.

All these workers-politicians were on the whole
experienced parliamentarians and could successfully
carry out the party's plan regarding the National
Assembly.   In 1968 this group, led by
J. Smrkovsky (originally a baker by profession),
proved quite conclusively to the Communist Party
and to the world that they were not only capable
of reviving this traditional Czechoslovak
institution, but also of making it into a decisive
political instrument in the conditions of the
Communist system.

The composition of the Federal Assembly and
National Councils in 1969-71 showed that the
reformers fully realised the importance of the
social composition of legislative Assemblies:

| Federal Assembly | 1969-71 | Czech Council | Slovak Council |
| --- | --- | --- | --- |
| Workers | 55 | 30 | 9 |
| Collective Farmers | 51 | 24 | 18 |
| Intelligentsia | 74 | 59 | 37 |
| Politicians | 147 | 56 | 56 |
| Army, Security | 12 | 1 | 3 |
| Retired, Housewives | 41 | 1 | 5 |

But after the 1971 election the social composition
was once again radically changed.   Though only
partial analyses are available, it is obvious that
worker representation predominates:   (North
Moravia region) 40.8 per cent workers from
factories, 14.4 per cent farmers and 21,4 per cent
intelligentsia which leaves only some 23 per cent
for politicians, presumably all those who had
survived the purges 1969-71.   This composition
seems to indicate that the Federal Assembly will
not be such an independent and powerful institution
as the National Assembly between 1964-8.   However,
it must also be pointed out that together with the
reforming deputies practically all the Stalinist

deputies, who had destroyed the old Assembly and hindered its revival, have left the Federal Assembly.

1. The chapter is entirely based on the Czechoslovak Hansard - Narodni shromazdeni republiky Ceskoslovenske - tesnopisecke zpravy o schuzich, Prague, 1945-1971.

# CHAPTER IV

## Central Government 1948-1968[1]

Preliminary Remarks

Since its inception in 1918, Czechoslovakia
has been governed by coalition government.  One
consequence of this arrangement was that cabinet
government or inner cabinet was not developed,
although it was tried for a short time.  The other
consequence was that the government has never
become too powerful;  it always contained uneasy
partners who put effective brakes to power
ambitions.  It was, rather, a platform for compromises and control over individual departments.
The government met as a body as was required (once
a week or month), made collective policy decisions
and controlled their execution.

Individual ministers, however, have always
exercised great powers.  Once the government had
made a compromise policy decision, it was the
minister's task to administer it.  He not only
supervised the administration of policies through
the civil servants, but also tried to avoid
control of his actions by his colleagues in
Parliament, or the President.  Controls not only
limited his power but also led to questions,
censures and political difficulties which usually
resulted in restriction and a crisis.  Not many
crises occurred between 1918 and 1948, and the last
one occurred on 20 February 1948, when members of
the government resigned in protest against police
measures taken by the Minister of the Interior,
V. Nosek, and sparked off the coup d'etat by the
Communist Party of Czechoslovakia.  Naturally, the
political composition of the government has always
been of primary importance.  Before the coup d'etat
non-Communist political parties controlled the
majority of the departments of state, of which the
government was composed.  In the first two
governments after World War II, the Prime Minister

was a Social Democratic Party leader, Z. Fierlinger, and non-Communists (including the two non-Party experts, Jan Masaryk and General Ludvik Svoboda, ministers of Foreign Affairs and Defence, respectively) controlled 15 out of the 22 ministries. After the election in 1946, the Communist leader, Klement Gottwald became Prime Minister, but the Communist Party continued to control only seven ministries out of 24. The coalition government continued its existence even after the coup d'etat, though the victory by the Communist Party was reflected in the composition of the government: it now controlled 13 ministries out of 22. Other political parties were given only token representation by the National Front: Social Democrats controlled four ministries; Czech Socialists two; Czech People's Party two; Slovak Revival Party one. Henceforth over the years even this token representation and sharing of power has declined and culminated in 1971, when the non-Communist parties failed to obtain any representation in the Federal government formed after the general election.

After the coup d'etat in 1948, the political control of ministries became much less important. The Communist Party now had an absolute majority in the government and, in any case, the ministers were chosen for their loyalty to the Communist Party, even the non-Communist members of the government. Moreover, the civil service as a professional body was abolished and ministries became curious political-administrative bodies executing policies decided upon at central committee meetings or Party praesidium sessions. It was no longer important who was the minister (Communist or non-Communist), for he made no decisions but only supervised the execution of policies by his staff. The officials responsible for the execution of policies were handpicked Communists, usually factory-workers, who were thought to be the most loyal Party members. They formed a local branch in the ministry and subjected it, and the minister, to the tightest political control. In practice, the local branch, which was

given the privileged status of a district committee,
controlled absolutely everything: the cadres,
appointments and administration of policies. Thus
the minister de facto lost control over his
ministry, officials and even the administration of
policies; he could not be blamed for failures, but
he could not gain any credit either. Ministers
were moved and sacked not because they were good or
bad administrators; their ministerial office
depended on their political standing within the
party (or parties).

Since the assumption of absolute power in
1948, the Communist Party of Czechoslovakia has not
solved the problem of political domination and
efficient administration. After 1948, the Communist
Party controlled absolutely central government as
the expression of its political victory. In 1960,
this was put right constitutionally and the Party
became the leading force in Czechoslovak society,
therefore the absolute ruler. However, the government never got back its powers of decision nor
professional civil service, and paradoxically
Czechoslovakia continued to be governed by a
coalition government whose policies had either
failed or had not been executed.

Civil Service

The disappearance of the professional civil
service was one reason for difficulties in central
administration. Another reason for difficulties
was the continuation of pre-coup practice of
appointing politicians as ministers who, in fact,
had become administrative heads. Even the most
capable administrators among these politicians
would have found it impossible to run central
ministries efficiently with the politically-reliable
but administratively unfit officials at their
disposal. The Communist Party was not content with
controlling absolutely the existing administration;
it decided to control practically everything, from
the economy to culture. This was well in line with
the Soviet model and the choice of central

123

ministries to achieve control was also typical. However, after 1950, when a whole host of ministries was established, central government and public administration in Czechoslovakia ground to a halt. Gradually the Communist Party became aware of this administrative collapse and quickly launched a series of reforms. Thus in 1953 a new ministry of State Control was established whose sole aim was to search for administrative problems and put them right. Significantly the new minister, K. Bacilek, was a former policeman and Minister of State Security, but the ministry failed to improve significantly the state administration, and was dissolved in 1960.

In 1953, the government itself tried to improve its working efficiency. It established a praesidium comprising the premier and his deputies whose function was to be a sort of inner cabinet. It was supposed to run the day-to-day affairs of the government between government sessions (roughly twice a month), co-orindate work of various ministries and generally improve administration. Thus it tried to re-establish the civil service by requiring educational qualifications from the newly established officials. Many workers were sent back to their factories, others moved from administrative tasks to clerical duties. However, the majority of the new men succeeded in gaining educational qualifications (e.g. from the Party High School), and they had to be left in their posts. Needless to say that such half-measures also failed to improve administrative efficiency.

In 1956, the Communist Party launched another reform: the planning and economic management was to be overhauled and a new economic administration introduced. However, the reform carried out between 1958 and 1960 also failed to dislodge the unqualified party officials and achieved nothing significant. In December 1964, the central committee decided on yet another reform: new cadre policies were to be applied to central government and on 1 January 1966 a new system of planning and economic management would come into effect. Even

124

in 1966 the problem of who should exercise power was not resolved: politically reliable technocrats still failed to replace political appointees and the reform would have failed completely had it not been for the events in 1968. Only in that year did the Communist Party come to the conclusion that without a professional civil service and administrative re-structuring Czechoslovakia could not be administered in the proper sense of the word.

Central Government

The programme of reform which the Communist Party of Czechoslovakia promulgated in April 1968 stated quite clearly that the existing executive arrangements were unsatisfactory. Thus the government's responsibility to the National Assembly and ministerial responsibility in general were insufficiently clear: "attempts were made to transfer ministerial responsibility to party organs and give up independent decision making. The government is not only the organ (executive) of economic policies. As the supreme organ of executive power it must concern itself as a whole with the entire gamut of political and administrative problems of the state. The government must also concern itself with the rational development of the entire state machinery. In the past, the machinery of state administration had been under-estimated; it is imperative that the machinery is run by qualified civil servants, is rationally developed, controlled by democratic means and above all made effective. Past simplifications, such as that national aims can be achieved by ignoring, or even weakening, the administrative apparatus, caused more damage than improvement". Substantial changes were demanded.

Constitutionally, the position of the government, as the chief executive organ, has not changed much since 1920. In the Socialist Constitution of 1960, Communist ideas on central government are outlined in Chapter V. While the descriptive parts are almost identical with those from the Soviet Constitution of 1936 (Chapter V, Articles 64-78), presidential and parliamentary provisions make Czechoslovak functional arrangements quite different from the Soviet ones. The government is appointed by the President on the recommendation of the National (Federal) Assembly and shares with him the power of appointment of higher civil servants, foreign service officials, university professors and higher army officers. Article 70 (para. 2) states unequivocally that "the government . . . goes about its tasks in the narrow co-operation and collaboration with the National Assembly and its organs".

The differences are quite significant and, in the past, they enabled Presidents Gottwald and Novotny, who were also party leaders, to dominate the executive both politically and administratively. As for the National Assembly, there has always been a meaningful co-operation between the executive and legislative, and the two branches of power have had a long and concrete experience of collaboration. The most persuasive demonstration of this co-operation is the fact that the President, on the whole, appoints ministers from the National Assembly rather than from the party apparatus. Although this practice has been modified and numerous exceptions made, it is still observed.

The constitutional amendments (Acts 77/1968Sb and 143/1968Sb), passed on 28 October 1968, which transformed Czechoslovakia into a federal republic, did not substantially alter the role of the government. Henceforth Czechoslovakia has, in fact, three governments, one federal and two republican, but their role as chief executive organs remains the same, only their competence is freshly delineated. The federal government's competence comprises (i) foreign affairs; (ii) defence; (iii) federal reserves, and (iv) federal legislation and constitutionalism. The Czech and Slovak governments consist of twelve ministries each, and eleven central administrations. The federal government shares competence with the two republican governments in the departments of (i) Planning; (ii) Finance; (iii) Prices; (iv) Trade, (v) Industry;

(vi) Agriculture; (vii) Transport; (viii) Post and
Telecommunications; (ix) Science and Technology; (x)
Labour, Wages and Social Security; (xi) Normalisation; (xii) Internal Order and Security, (xiii)
Press and Information.  Since 1 January 1969, when
the federal constitution came into effect, the
structure and competence of government became more
complex, but otherwise little different.  In the new
scheme, the President appoints the federal government on the recommendation of the Federal Assembly;
the republican governments are appointed by the
Speakers of the Czech and Slovak National Councils
which co-operate with the national governments in
the close, traditional way.


Government Composition

        When in February 1948 the Communist Party
achieved an absolute majority in the coalition
government (13 ministries out of 22), the other
political parties were not banned from government:
the coalition continued in tact.  While the Czech
Socialist Party and People's Party suffered heavy
losses (they each lost a Deputy Premiership), the
Social Democrats actually improved their position in
the government: they not only held on to the Deputy
Premiership (B. Lausman), but also controlled the
ministry of Industry (Z. Fierlinger), Social Security
(E. Erban) and Food (L. Jankovcova).  At this stage,
Gottwald still presided over a coalition government
composed of politicians (party leaders) whose
policies were decided by the government itself and
executed by the civil service.  After the election
in May 1948, and resignation of President Benes, the
government of February 1948 also stood down.
Gottwald was elected unanimously President of the
Czechoslovak Republic and A. Zapotocky succeeded
him as Prime Minister.  On 15 June 1948, on the
recommendation of the National Assembly, President
Gottwald appointed a new government, headed by his
old political friend and chairman of the Czechoslovak
Central Unions Council, Antonin Zapotocky.  It was,
once again, a coalition government, but the non-
Communist representation decreased still further.

127

# CZECHOSLOVAK GOVERNMENT
## 15.6.1948-12.12,1954

### Prime Minister

A. Zapotocky:  from 21.3.1953 V. Siroky

### Deputies

V. Siroky

Z. Fierlinger
(to  14.9.1953)

J. Sevcik
(Slovak Revival Party)
(to  30.5.1952)

V. Kopecky

L. Svoboda
(from 25.4.1950-8.9.1951)

R. Slansky
(from 8.9.1951-24.11.1951)

J.  Dolansky

J. Kysely
(Slovak Revival Party)
(6.6.1952-31.1.1953)

A. Novotny
(from 31.1.1953-14,9,1953)

Z. Nejedly

K. Bacilek

J. Uher

A. Cepicka

O. Beran

R. Barak

(continued)

## CZECHOSLOVAK GOVERNMENT

| | |
|---|---|
| Foreign Affairs: | V. Clemtis; V. Siroky; V. David |
| Defence: | L. Svoboda; A. Cepicka |
| Foreign Trade: | A. Gregor; R. Dvorak |
| Interior: | V. Nosek; R. Barak |
| Finance: | J. Dolansky; J. Kabes; J. Duris |
| Education: | Z. Nejedly; E. Sykora; L. Stoll |
| Justice: | A. Cepicka; S. Rais; V. Skoda |
| Information: | V. Kopecky |
| Industry: | G. Kliment; J. Maurer; K. Polacek |
| Agriculture: | J. Duris; J. Nepomucky; J. Uher |
| Trade: | F. Krajcir |
| Transport: | A. Petr; A. Pospisil (both Czech People's Party) |
| Post and Communications: | A. Neuman (Czech Socialist Party) |
| Social Security: | E. Erban; J. Havelka; V. Nosek |
| Health: | J. Plojhar (Czech People's Party) |
| Food: | L. Jankovcova |

(continued)

## CZECHOSLOVAK GOVERNMENT

| | |
|---|---|
| Technology: | E. Slechta (Czech Socialist Party) to 20.12.1950 |
| Law Unification: | V. Srobar (Slovak Revival Party) to 6.12.1950 |
| State Planning Commission: | J. Dolansky; J. Pucik; O. Simunek |
| National Security: | L. Kopriva; K. Bacilek |
| Light Industry: | J. Jonas; A. Malek |
| Building Industry: | E. Slechta (Czech Socialist Party) |
| Fuel and Energy: | V. Pokorny; J. Jonas |
| State Control: | K. Bacilek; J. Harus; O. Beran |
| Furnaces, Iron Ore Mines: | J. Bilek; J. Reitmajer |
| General Engineering: | J. Jonas |
| Forests and Wood Industry: | M. Smida; J. Duris; M. Simda |
| Chemical Industry: | J. Pucik; O. Simunek; J. Pucik |
| Railways: | J. Pospisil |
| Purchases: | J. Krosnar |
| Universities: | L. Stoll |
| Building Materials: | J. Kysely (Slovak Revival Party) |
| State Farms: | M. Smida |

(continued)

## CZECHOSLOVAK GOVERNMENT

| | |
|---|---|
| Energy: | B. Sramek |
| Local Economy: | J. Kysely (Slovak Revival Party) |
| Culture: | V. Kopecky |
| Ministers: | J. Maurer; Z. Nejedly |
| SC of Art: | J. Taufer |
| SC of Cultural Relations with Foreign Countries: | J. Urban |

---

Shortly after the election the Social Democrats joined the Communist Party and ceased to be represented in the government separately. The Czech Socialists were given the ministries of Post (A. Neuman) and Technology (Professor E. Slechta), while the People's Party controlled the ministries of Transport (A. Petr) and Health (Reverend J. Plojhar). A lonely Slovak Revival Party member, V. Srobar, headed the ministry of Law Unification until 1950, when it was dissolved.

Although the Communist Party now controlled the government absolutely, and the Premier Zapotocky was second to the party leader Gottwald, the latter took in fact the government firmly into his own hands, and created a kind of presidential regime. In Czechoslovakia, this was not such an unusual arrangement: in the past, during emergencies and crises, Presidents Masaryk and Benes also established such arrangements. What was more significant, at this stage, was Gottwald's fusion of the presidential and party offices. After 1949, when Gottwald could dispense with the services of the National Assembly, and had time to build up a parallel party, party to everything else in the

131

state, he could govern directly without anybody
else. The power of the Prime Minister evaporated
and that of the ministers soon went as well.

So far, members of the government were also
parliamentary deputies and were appointed by the
President as ministers from the National Assembly.
By 1950, Gottwald took to appointing as he pleased:
He dismissed General Svoboda as Defence Minister
and appointed his Minister of Justice in his stead.
Contrary to constitutional usage, he appointed
S. Rais as Minister of Justice, although he was not
a member of parliament, and was, in fact, a civil
servant from the Presidential Chancellory. Subsequently, Gottwald made many similar appointments,
especially to the newly established economic
ministries. By then the government was reduced to
the status of the civil service pure and simple, for
it also ceased to make its own policy decisions,
which were taken over by party organs (mainly
departments of the central committee) and finalised
by the President himself.

This new practice of ministerial appointments
was strongly disliked even in the Communist Party,
though no one dared to object to it. Party leaders
expected ministerial appointments for party loyalty
and work. Gottwald, who probably fully-appreciated
the change of role of the government, refused to
appoint his party colleagues to ministerial jobs,
and stuck to his decision as long as he lived. Thus
in 1949, when he established another ministry, the
State Planning Commission, he made his finance
minister, Professor J. Dolansky, its first head.
At this stage, Dolansky's position within the
Communist Party was not particularly strong, but
subsequent leaders could not do without his expert
knowledge and experience, and he ended up as the
most unlikely member of the party praesidium under
President Novotny. He was replaced in the ministry
of Finance by J. Kabes, whose standing in the party
was no greater. Similarly, the minister of Education,
Z. Nejedly, a party praesidium member, was replaced
by E. Sykora, without equivalent party standing:
minister of Heavy Industry became J. Maurer; Dolansky

was later replaced by J. Pucik, a technocrat rather than a politician.

Gottwald still further reduced the power of the executive by frequent reorganisations. In 1949, after he had created the Central Planning Commission, he transformed the various branches of industry into ministries. In 1950, the ministry of Industry, which up to then administered all the industries in Czechoslovakia, became the ministry of Heavy Industry (subsequently of Heavy Engineering) and, at the same time, he set up a ministry of Light Industry. (The minister, J. Jonas, was again more a technocrat than a political leader.) The ministry of Technology, run by the Czech Socialist minister, Professor Slechta, was dissolved and a new ministry of Building was set up for him. A year later, ministries of Fuel and Energy, Furnaces and Ore Mines, General Engineering, Forests and Wood Industry, as well as Chemical Industries, were established and all went to technocrats rather than politicians-praesidium members: L. Kopriva became the minister of State Security and K. Bacilek, minister of State Control. Gottwald added a few ministries to the government in 1952: ministry of Railways (J. Pospisil) and ministry of Agricultural Purchases (J. Krosnar), but early in 1953, just before his death, he re-organised the government so thoroughly that it came to resemble almost completely the Soviet government. Ministries and state commit-tees (with ministerial status) were created even in fields where there was nothing to administer in Czechoslovakia. Thus the ministry of Universities (L. Stoll) lasted exactly seven months; similarly the ministries of Building Materials (J. Kysely), State Farms (M. Smida), Energy (B. Sramek), Committee for Arts (J. Taufer) and Committee of Cultural Relations with Foreign Countries (J. Urban). Since all these ministries were headed by politicians it is just possible that Gottwald finally gave way to their pressure. At the time of Gottwald's death the government of Czechoslovakia consisted of 36 ministries and in size rivalled with the Soviet government, although perhaps it was not exactly proportionate to the population and economic wealth of Czechoslovakia.

Despite Gottwald's predilection for technocrats, the steady expansion of the state
apparatus (central and regional administration)
between 1948-1953 took care of ambitious party
leaders, if Gottwald's purges failed to take care
of them. Gottwald dispensed with all the
formalities, held no elections, no government
presented its programme or account to the National
Assembly, and the ministries were the safest jobs,
except for re-shuffles and re-organisations. It
was most disconcerting, for example, for such an
ambitious leader as J. Duris to find himself
without a ministry reflecting his party status
after one of these re-organisations. Still with
Gottwald's death all this was bound to come to an
end, for there was no strong personality left in
the Communist Party to carry on.

It took the Communist Party six months to
plan its new policies. In September 1953, a whole
series of ministries and state committees was
dissolved. But the most significant reform was
contained in the governmental order 5/1953 by
which the work of the government itself was regulated. Until then, at least according to constitutional usage, the government was a collective body
which made its decisions at regular (weekly)
meetings and controlled their implementation subsequently. In 1953, Soviet constitutional
arrangements were copied: the Prime Minister and
his deputies formed a praesidium (a sort of inner
cabinet) which alone had the powers of decision;
it also carried on the business of the government
in between meetings which were now spaced at
greater intervals (monthly). This reform was
supposed to make the government work really
effectively and strengthen the executive considerably. However, the reform failed for the
Czechoslovak politicians were unused to this
arrangement and did not know how to work it. The
government's powers were strengthened, nevertheless,
but for the simple reason that the new President,
A. Zapotocky, insisted on being a constitutional

Prime Minister
V. Siroky

1st Deputy
J. Dolansky
A. Cepicka

Deputies
V. Kopecky
L. Jankovcova
V. Skoda
K. Polacek
R. Barak
O. Simunek

| | |
|---|---|
| Interior: | R. Barak |
| Defence: | A. Cepicka; B. Lomsky |
| Planning Commission: | O. Simunek |
| Local Economy: | J. Kysely (Slovak Revival Party) |
| Health: | J. Plojhar (Czech People's Party) |
| Building: | E. Slechta (Czech Socialist Party); O. Beran |
| Foreign Affairs: | V. David |
| Finance: | J. Duris |
| Trade: | F. Krajcir; L. Brabec |

(continued)

## CZECHOSLOVAK GOVERNMENT

| | |
|---|---|
| Forests, Wood Industry: | J. Krosnar |
| Purchases: | B. Machacova-Dotsalova |
| Engineering: | K. Polacek; J. Bukal; J. Reitmajer |
| Culture: | L. Stoll |
| Food Industry: | J. Uher |
| State Control: | O. Beran; M. Bakula; J. Krosnar |
| Fuel and Energy: | J. Jonas |
| Furnaces, Iron Ore Mines: | J. Reitmajer; V. Cerny |
| Agriculture: | M. Smida; V. Krutina; M. Bakula; L. Strougal |
| Justice: | J. Baturska; V. Skoda |
| Foreign Trade: | R. Dvorak; F. Krajcir |
| Education: | F. Kahuda |
| Light Industry: | A. Malek; B. Machacova-Dostalova |
| Communication: | A. Neuman (Czech Socialist Party) |
| Labour Force: | V. Nosek |
| Transport: | A. Pospisil (Czech People's Party); F. Vlasak |
| Chemical Industry: | J. Pucik |
| Energy: | F. Vlasak; A. Pospisil (Czech People's Party) |

(continued)

## CZECHOSLOVAK GOVERNMENT

| | |
|---|---|
| Exact Engineering: | V. Ouzky |
| Car Industry and Agricultural Machinery: | E. Zatloukal |
| State Farms: | M. Smida |
| SC of Building: | O. Beran; E Slechta (Czech Socialist Party) |
| SC of Development of Wood, Water, etc. | J. Kysely (Slovak Revival Party) |
| General Engineering: | K. Polacek |
| SC of Development of Technology: | V. Ouzky |
| Ministers: | Z. Nejedly; J. Maurer; J. Tesla; V. Ouzky |

---

figurehead and refused to assume the chairmanship of the Communist Party thus separating the
two powerful positions. Thus between 1953 and
1957, it seemed that the government would recover
its former powers and constitutional position, and
more efficient administration of Czechoslovakia
would be resumed.

However, even this new system of collective
leadership failed to bring about the desired aims.
The newly formed government and its ministries
continued to act as in the past, refused to
accept responsibility and tried to cope with
operational problems by hiring more personnel.
They succeeded in pushing responsibility for
failure from themselves onto the Planning Commission
or on the governmental praesidium which allegedly
made decisions no ministry could implement. It was
the old vicious circle again and in 1955 yet another

# CZECHOSLOVAK GOVERNMENT
## appointed 11.7.1960

### Prime Minister
V. Siroky

### Deputies
O. Simunek
(Plan)

J. Piller

F. Krajcir

O. Cernik

A. Indra

| | |
|---|---|
| Interior: | L. Strougal |
| Fuel and Energy: | O. Cernik |
| Foreign Affairs: | V. David |
| Foreign Trade: | F. Krajcir |
| Finance: | J. Duris |
| Defence: | B. Lomsky |
| Consumer Industries: | B. Machacova-Dostalova |
| People's Control: | J. Krosnar |
| Justice: | A. Neuman (Czech Socialist Party) |
| Health: | J. Plojhar (Czech People's Party) |
| General Engineering: | K. Polacek |
| Agriculture: | V. Krutina |

(continued)

## CZECHOSLOVAK GOVERNMENT

| | |
|---|---|
| Food Industries: | J. Uher |
| Building: | O. Beran |
| Education and Culture: | F. Kahuda |
| Heavy Engineering: | J. Reitmajer |
| Transport: | F. Vlasak |
| Chemical Industries: | J. Pucik |
| Trade: | L. Brabec |
| Furnaces, Iron Ore Mines: | N. Smok |
| SC for the Development of Science: | J. Dolansky |
| Ministers: | J. Korcak (Central Energy Administration); M. Chudik, V. Krahulec |

---

re-organisation was ordered (Order 48/1955). Then suddenly in 1956 many of the reforms of 1955 were cancelled and instead new ministries were established. The government reversed its ruling on the established posts in the civil services: civil servants who had required educational qualifications but proved 'unsuccessful' were dismissed and the unqualified 'political' civil servants were re-established provided that they were able to acquire some sort of a degree, usually from a party school or institution.

President Zapotocky's virtual resignation from power brought forward the administrative head of the Communist Party, Antonin Novotny. In 1953 he was for some six months deputy Prime Minister, but otherwise his experience was the party. When, however, in 1957, Zapotocky died, Novotny had himself elected President of Czechoslovakia and once again fused the offices of President and head of the Communist Party. Even such short a term as Deputy Premier convinced Novotny that the executive had to be revived somehow and he and the party devised several new schemes between 1958 and 1960. Though they were all supposed to simplify central administration, introduce new planning methods in the economy, they invariably had the opposite effect from the intended one. Perhaps as a result of past errors, and certainly as a consequence of administrative malfunctioning, Czechoslovakia was in the grip of an economic recession between 1962 and 1964. In 1965, one more system of planning and administration was devised and passed by the Communist Party. The new system came into effect on 1 January 1966 and was supposed to modernise everything, the economy, administration and planning. It even contained provisions against the misuse of the new methods by local administrators. Though it was too soon to see the final results of this reform, the experiment was not proceeding satisfac- torily. The events in 1968 interrupted the reform which was proclaimed insufficient and the subsequent re-organisation of central administration and government on federal lines finally ended it.


Government Structures

        Throughout the period 1948-1968, a sustained growth of the administrative machine was recorded. In 1948, Czechoslovakia was administered through 18 ministries; by 1953 their number rose to 38. Though a number of ministries was abolished after Gottwald's death, the reforms in 1955-6 resurrected many of them - some became state committees, others central administrations. In 1967, after another reform, the government controlled directly the following state committees and central administrations: (i) State Planning Commission; (ii) Commission for Classification of Mineral Resources; (iii) Research Institute of Economic Planning; (iv) State Statistical Office; (v) Slovak Statistical Office;

## CZECHOSLOVAK GOVERNMENT
appointed on 20.9.1963-1968

### Prime Minister
J. Lenart

### Deputies
O. Simunek

J. Piller

F. Krajcir

O. Cernik

| | |
|---|---|
| Interior: | L. Strougal; J. Kudrna |
| Energy: | J. Odvarka |
| Foreign Affairs: | V. David |
| Foreign Trade: | F. Hamouz |
| Finance: | R. Dvorak |
| Defence: | B. Lomsky |
| Consumer Industries: | B. Machacova-Dostalova |
| SC of Control: | P. Majling |
| Justice: | A. Neuman (Czech Socialist Party) |
| Health: | J. Plojhar (Czech People's Party) |
| General Engineering: | K. Polacek |
| Agriculture: | J. Burian |
| Food Industries: | V. Krutina |

(continued)

141

## CZECHOSLOVAK GOVERNMENT

| | |
|---|---|
| Building: | S. Takac |
| Education: | O. Cisar |
| Heavy Engineering: | J. Pesl |
| Transport: | A. Indra |
| Chemical Industries: | J. Pucik |
| Trade: | J. Uher |
| Furnaces, Iron Ore Mines: | J. Krejci |
| SC of Development and Co-ordination of Science: | F. Vlasak |
| Ministers: | J. Korcak (Central Energy Administration); M. Chudik; V. Krahulec |

---

(vi) Research Institute of Control, Evidence and
Statistics; (vii) State Commission of Direction and
Organisation (with the Institute of Management and
the Institute of State Administration); (viii)
State Commission of Technology (with the Office of
Normalisation and Measures, Meteorological Office,
Institute of Electro Technology, Institute of
Engineering, Office of Patents and Inventions,
Institute of Radioisotopes, Institute of Material
Manipulation, Institute of Accountancy and Auto-
mation, Research Institute of Building and Archi-
tecture, State Institute of Regional Planning,
Institute of Typology, Central Office of Science,
Technology and Economic Information, Research
Institute of Economics and Development, as well as
the Czechoslovak Commission of Atomic Energy); (ix)
State Commission of Finance, Prices and wages, and
finally (x) the Central Commission of People's
Control.

142

Each ministry also had several central administrations under its jurisdiction. Thus the
ministry of Finance included the Research Institute
of Finance, Czechoslovak Commercial Bank, Investment
Bank, Central Office of Property and Currency, State
Insurance Office, Central Administration of Savings
Banks, the Trade Bank, the State Bank of
Czechoslovakia and the State Mint. Industrial
ministries were regular monsters: thus the ministry
of Mining administered in addition to all the coal
mines, uranium mines, gas production, iron ore mines,
also the Central Office of Geology, Institute of
Applied Geophysics and many other administrations
and institutes. The ministry of Transport, for
example,(established by a parliamentary praesidium's
decree 3 in 1963) administered, apart from all the
railways, river shipping and air transport, some 31
other administrations and research establishments.
The ministry of Trade which was established in 1945
(presidential decree 1/1945), chiefly to help with
the reconstruction of shops, wholesale businesses
and also with controlling prices, was by 1967 a
super-ministry with 10 research institutes and
central administrations, all the shops in
Czechoslovakia, as well as tourism, hotels and all
the other services. The ministry of Foreign Trade
has the monopoly of exports and controls 36 export
corporations, research institutes, customs and
excise, and all the chambers of commerce. The
ministry of Health, which has also grown considerably since its establishment in 1945, controls 33
research institutes, 18 spas, as well as the
entire pharmaceutical industry, doctors, hospitals,
nurses and a supply system. Only the ministry of
Education does not seem to have grown out of all
proportion: it administers schools and universities
adding to its responsibilities only the occasional
research institute. In contrast, the ministry of
Culture and Information (established by the
parliamentary praesidium's decree 1/1967) administers all cultural activity in Czechoslovakia: book
publishing, theatres, museums, art galleries,
concerts, authors copyright, the press, cultural
relations with foreign countries, and also protects
nature and churches. Film production and film

making, as well as the Czechoslovak Press Agency
are included together with broadcasting, television and the Academy of Sciences.

Some traditional ministries, such as the
ministry of Foreign Affairs, Internal Affairs,
Defence and Justice, after many reforms still
retained their structures more or less in tact
and have not grown excessively, However, a whole
series of untraditional central administrations
was established to accomplish specific tasks. In
1954 (governmental decree 20/1954) the Central
Mining Office was founded to supervise the
implementation of the mining law passed three
years later (Act 41/1957Sb). In 1966, the Central
Publications Administration came into being (Act
81/1966Sb); it was in fact the central censorship
office co-ordinating the supervision of all the
communication media so that "no state, economic
and army secrets were published" (a sort of moral
censorship were made public. Other central administrations, such as the Central Commission of
Workers' Education, State Commission of Science
Degrees, State Population Commission, State
Committee of Tourism, etc. were usually attached
to various ministries and staffed by them. With
the federal arrangements coming into force in 1969,
central administration was made even more complex:
the two republics are administered by separate
governments and federal ministries administer
federal affairs. Though certain modifications have
already been envisaged the structure of central
administration and government in Czechoslovakia
still remain as huge, complex and impressive as
those of the USSR.


Decision Making

Traditionally, Czechoslovakia had a government
which met regularly (every week or so), made
collective policy decisions which were then implemented by individual departments of state ministries.
After the coup d'etat in 1948, this practice was
gradually discontinued, however the Soviet practice

of holding joint government and Communist Party
praesidium meetings (and issuing government/central
committee policy statements) has never been
imitated and never came into use. During the
personality cult period, President Gottwald found
it easier to issue instructions from his office to
individual ministries, and ultimately came to make
all the government decisions himself as the leader.
After Gottwald's death, Czechoslovakia began to
imitate the USSR a little: government meetings were
held after central committee sessions and policy
statements were simply re-iterated in more administrative terms. However, the period 1953-8 was
rather confused and it is almost impossible to
determine how government policies were formulated
and how decisions were made.

Only after 1958, it began to be clear how the
system worked: by this time the Presidency and the
party leadership were fused again, but Novotny was
no Gottwald. Though he used some of Gottwald's
methods he could not use them all, thus condemning
his system to failure in advance. On 21 January
1958, President Novotny reported to the central
committee of the Communist Party of Czechoslovakia
on the Communist summit meeting in Moscow. Almost
simultaneously the Czechoslovak government announced
its position on the atom free zone in Central
Europe, a matter discussed both in Moscow and in
the central committee. At another meeting of the
central committee, on 27 and 28 February 1958, new
arrangements for finance, planning in industry, and
building, as well as the economic effects of
investments were discussed. On 16 March 1958, the
government announced its own plans for a new organisation of industry which were coming into force on
1 April 1958: this shows quite conclusively that
the re-organisation was prepared and sanctioned by
the Communist Party (or better still by the 1st
Secretary and President). On 16 June 1958, the
central committee announced its own measures for
increased efficiency of the local economy; the
government responded by announcing the same concrete
measures on 11 July. It also ordered improvements
in the organisation of the coming harvest with which

145

the central committee had not dealt.  Between 19
and 22 June 1958, the 11th Congress of the Communist
Party of Czechoslovakia took place; it discussed the
new Five Year Plan and approved the concrete proposals laid before it by the praesidium.  On 1st
August 1958, the government made public new targets
for the Five Year Plan and also approved organisational changes discussed by the Congress.  It is
not at all clear who had prepared the economic plan;
it is clear that the Congress of the Communist Party
had made final decisions and that the
government undertook to execute the plan.

In 1959, this pattern of decision making
became a regular feature of the government's work.
On 7 March 1959 the central  committee approved an
increase in child allowances, a decrease in shop
prices, increase in pensions and a cut in working
hours.  Exactly the same announcements were made by
the government on the same day giving them legal
force.  However, the April session of the central
committee in 1959 was not followed by identical
government announcements: the new agricultural
purchase system as well as the new prices of
agricultural produce were dealt with by the government in August, September and October 1959, when
finally concrete matters as agricultural purchases
and prices the government was given a free hand
and that it worked out its own schemes and
measures.  The Five Year Plan, which the central
committee discussed both in April and September
1959, was also dealt with by the government in July
and December 1959.  The evident lag of government
measures behind the central committee decisions
was undoubtedly due to the difficulty of translating
the more general decisions into concrete
administrative terms.

In 1960, the government announced its budget
on 18 February 1960, long before the session of
the central committee, which took place in April
1960.  Undoubtedly, this was due to the party's
pre-occupation with the new constitution.  On the
other hand, the government was still clearing up
the backlog of party decisions from 1959:  it

announced reforms of the collective farms, improvements in agricultural machinery as well as the
reduction of shop prices, together with free school
books and other social measures. The April session
of the central committee discussed the new
constitution and increased powers of local government. It probably also approved a general amnesty
- convicted party leaders, Dr Husak among them,
were finally released from prisons and concentration camps - which the President proclaimed on 9
May 1960.

In June 1960, the government proclaimed the
reforms of local government whose powers, in
particular the financial ones, were considerably
increased, and made the reform effective henceforth.
It is obvious that it accepted the project of the
reform from the Communist Party. In July 1960, the
central committee dealt in addition to the
constitution with the Five Year Plan, agriculture
and probably also with the composition of the new
government which was appointed after the general
election. Premier Siroky continued in the office
and only very few changes were made, non of them
politically significant. The new government dealt
with the economy and the plan on 7 August 1960. In
October 1960, the government implemented two
measures previously decided upon by the central
committee: university appointments and finance was
newly regulated. In addition, wages in the building
industry were increased and a new way of financing
house building was devised. Perhaps a little
paradoxically on 23 October 1960 the recently
strengthened local government saw some of the local
taxes abolished. The government took no action,
not even in 1961, on central committee decisions
arrived at in December 1960: another re-organisation
of chemical industry was announced together with the
'renovation' of socialist legality.

In 1961, perhaps surprising it was the turn
of the central committee to react to government
plans and measures rather than anticipating them.
In February 1961, the central committee dealt with
such blanket subjects as agriculture, building and

147

railways; no concrete decisions were made. On the other hand, in June 1961, the government announced an increased building programme and improvements in agricultural production. The June session of the central committee backed up these measures by ordering the district administration and district party committees to help directly in the villages. In September 1961, the party tried again to buttress the government measures announcing the formation of a new university, as well as new arrangements for part-time students. Subsequently the central committee announced its intentions of making national education a truly Communist one: it also decided to increase party propaganda in educational establishments. At the November session the central committee dealt with the youth as a whole, and in particular endorsed the government measures concerning the universities.

In 1962, the Communist Party devoted most of its attention to the preparation of the crucial 12th Congress, and only one session, in February 1962, was devoted to problems in the economy and agriculture. In contrast, the government appeared very busy running the economy and agriculture. In January 1962, it announced additional measures for the improvement of agricultural production. In February 1962, new labour norms came into effect, and preventative measures against mining accidents were taken. The film industry was reorganised, agricultural purchases were modified and a new State Committee of Development was set up. In March 1962, additional measures were taken to organise agricultural work more effectively and in June 1962 concrete plans for dealing with the harvest were announced. Previously the government increased collective farmers' social security and pensions and it was no surprise that the Five Year Plan was being fulfilled satisfactorily. In July 1962, the government dealt with transport problems and in August with the harvest as well as public health. In September 1962, the government approved the planning targets and prepared the budget which were then discussed and passed in the National Assembly.

The 12th Congress of the Communist Party of Czechoslovakia was a turning point, which meant a break with many past practices. The relations between the central committee and the government were newly regulated: so far apparently party organs were supplanting central administration and, as a consequence, no one was willing to make decisions and accept responsibility for them. Failures of, and deficiency in, central administration were attributed to the Communist Party and this could not continue. The praesidium decided on a radical change: new men were needed to carry out new policies. In a major re-shuffle, Premier V. Siroky, together with a number of political ministers, (Duris, Krosnar, Kahuda, but also Strougal), were dismissed and the new government under the youthful J. Lenart introduced the new ways of administration. The government was to receive from the Communist Party only long term and general instructions, and even these directives were to be prepared central committee commissions especially established for this purpose. The commissions were to work out 'conceptual problems' (economic, agricultural, ideological, etc.), have them approved by the central committee which would then pass them on to the government for implementation. It was also suggested that new statutes should be worked out for individual ministries so that they also could carry out their administrative tasks in a new way. To improve administration still further, it was suggested to re-introduce individual responsibility into administrative work, streamline the structures and cut personnel.

Henceforth, apart from annual budgets and some urgent proclamations (eg. "save electricity") no publicity was given to joint central committee and government meetings and decisions. In 1964, the central committee dealt with economic development and living standards: on 7 February the government announced concrete measures in both respects. In April 1964, the government presented its budget, while the central committee dealt with cultural matters. In 1966, there was only one joint

party-government statement and it concerned the
Communist Summit Meeting at Bucharest. In 1967,
there were no joint statements at all, while the
central committee discussed a whole gamut of
general problems: youth, agriculture, local
government, economic plan and balance, living
standards, general election in 1968, etc. It is
probably that the party in-fighting and struggle
for the leadership left the government relatively
free to tackle national problems and administer
the country. All the same, in April 1968,
Premier Lenart was dismissed and accused of
carrying out blindly party directives instead of
governing and administering Czechoslovakia.

In 1968, in the programme of action, new
working arrangements between the Communist Party
and the government were established. Although
the party praesidium and central committee still
reserved for themselves the right to proclaim
policies as a guidance for the government, the
executive would otherwise be left free to
govern and administer the country. The Communist
Party moreover would only issue general policy
statements prepared after exhaustive consultations
with party commissions and the National Front,
which includes other political parties as well as
interest groups. It is clear that the government
of Czechoslovakia was firmly re-established;
however, before these new arrangements could be
properly tested, Czechoslovakia was occupied by
the armies of the Warsaw Pact, and it seems that
after 1969 it reverted to the old arrangements of
sporadic party intervention.


Ministry of Defence: A Case Study

If in the past twenty years the central
government was treated in such an untraditional
manner and was greatly reduced in its constitutional standing and power, individual ministries
did not fare differently. Since, however, the
Presidents and party leaders could not dominate
them as easily as the government as a whole,

they often succeeded in reversing the downgrading
trend and were able to return to the pre-1948
structural and functional arrangements. The
Ministry of Defence is perhaps the best example of
this process. After all, Czechoslovakia accumulated long experience and a sound administrative
tradition in the defence field. After 1918, the
French mission modified in some respects the army
organisation inherited from the Habsburg Monarchy,
but overall administrative arrangements were left
in tact. A politician ran the ministry of Defence
by means of ministerial departments and the
general staff; an inter-ministerial council
proved particularly effective with procurement
policies and, as a result, the Czechoslovak army
was the best equipped force in Central Europe and
at a reasonable cost.

In 1945, when Czechoslovakia was re-established, the ministry of Defence was also rebuilt
in the traditional way despite the fact that the
armies and air forces were heterogeneous and
organised in all sorts of ways (British and Soviet
chiefly). The Minister of Defence, General L.
Svoboda, who had fought in the USSR and had also
had close contacts with Czechoslovak Communist
leaders, was responsible for the decision to
rebuild the old system. Instead of the Soviet
military councils he re-formed the old ministerial
departments: the 1st administered general military
affairs, the 3rd was the economic administration
and the 5th looked after the air force and the 6th
after army health. The General Staff also retained
its traditional five sections: 1st organisation;
2nd (deuxieme bureau) intelligence; 3rd operations.
In 1945, on joining the government of Czechoslovakia,
the Communist Party insisted on the establishment
of two new departments which it held under its
own strict supervision. The department of Education
and Enlightenment might have been thought as Branch
B of the old system, but in fact it was a direct
imitation of the Soviet political system. Major
(later Lieutenant General), J. Prochazka, who was
put in charge of this department, was an experienced
Communist Party leader who knew that this department
could neutralise the army if it became mixed in

political struggle. The other new department of counter-espionage (HSOZ) was headed by Major B. Reicin, another Communist, and was to be used to destroy the army, if it actually acted against the Communist Party. With these two 'insurance' departments under its control, the Communist Party permitted the re-building of the ministry, the inter-ministerial military council, supreme council of state defence and the army consultative council.

After the coup d'etat in 1948, the Communist Party did not think it necessary to treat the ministry of Defence harshly. The minister of Defence finally joined the Communist Party and a few officers were purged for their pronounced anti-Communist views. Until 1950, General Svoboda succeeded in keeping both the ministry and the army in tact and did not require Soviet military advisors. He even dared to suggest in the government that Czechoslovakia should purchase military equipment in the West, since it could not obtain it from the USSR. But in 1950, President Gottwald decided on a complete re-organisation of the ministry and armies and appointed his son-in-law, Dr. A. Cepicka, to carry it out. The new minister of Defence immediately purged the ministry and the army of Svoboda's officers and staff and began the re-organisation: the Czechoslovak army had to be transformed into a complete imitation of the Soviet army in both training and equipment and he called for Soviet advisors to help him. The ministry was to be re-organised as well and here he needed Soviet advisors as well. Cepicka abolished the supreme council of state defence in 1950 and in 1951 the army consultative council. In their stead he set up something unique, neither Soviet nor Czechoslovak, the Military Council.

The Military Council was responsible for all the defence matters and began to meet once a month. Cepicka acted as chairman, his two deputy defence ministers, General Lastovicka (a journalist by profession) and General Hruska responsible for political education, were members of the council as well as General Prochazka, former Politruk, now Chief of Staff, and ministerial secretary (at first

Colonel J. Strasil and, subsequently, Colonel J.
Sejna, who sought political a sylum in the West
in 1968). From the beginning, an equivalent
number of Soviet advisors attended the council
meetings and undoubtedly dispensed advice. After
1954, the Soviet advisors attended the meeting as
visitors and in 1956 the council was wound up
and replaced by the traditional army consultative
council. However, apart from this innovation
Cepicka succeeded only in dis-organising the army
which was completely transformed. The Political
Administration (formerly a section of the general
staff) was built up and became the department of
the central committee of the Communist Party. Its
head was one of the deputy defence ministers and
member of the central committee. In 1956, Cepicka
was dismissed and his successor, General B. Lomsky
started the long haul of re-establishing the
ministry and the army. Thus his deputy ministers
were in fact in charge of the old departments and
the general staff. The head of the Political
Administration remained deputy defence minister
so that the military had him under better control.
By 1968, General Lomsky made such a good progress
in re-establishing his ministry and the army that
no great changes were necessary to make the
ministry acceptable to the new leaders. Though
L msky was also dismissed for political reasons
(apparently he was implicated in a plan to use the
army in support of President Novotny), the only
change carried out in 1968 was the creation of
the Council of State Defence, which in many ways
resembles the old Supreme Council of State Defence.
Thus although the Czechoslovak army in training,
discipline and equipment is identical with the
Soviet army (and the armies of the Warsaw Pact),
in the administration of defence Czechoslovakia is
back to traditional arrangements.

The ministry of Defence's development is not
unique; other ministries went through disruptive
experiences only to return to the traditional way
of organising things. In 1951, a new Ministry of
National Security was set up to cope with security;
immediately after Gottwald's death it was abolished

and the Ministry of the Interior resumed its
responsibility for security (2nd department).
After experiments, the administration of education, science and culture in Czechoslovakia came
under the traditional ministries of Education
(with science and research included) and culture.
Even in the case of industrial ministries where
there is no tradition the tendency is to act as
top co-ordinating bodies rather than rigid,
centralised bureaucracies. However, it is quite
clear that the Communist way of running the
government and ministries impaired their effect-
iveness and efficiency.

## MILITARY COUNCIL
### (1951-6)

Composition

Minister
A. Cepicka

Chief Soviet Advisor
Gen. Gusev

Chief of Staff
Gen. Prochazka

Chief of Staff Advisor
Gen. Zherebin

Politruk
Gen. Hruska

Politruk Advisor
Gen. Sidykh

Deputy Minister
Gen. Lastovicka

Soviet Advisor
Gen. Byelik

## MINISTRY OF DEFENCE
### (1967)

Minister                    Gen. B. Lomsky (1956-68)

Deputy Ministers            Gen. V. Janko (Personnel)

                            Gen. J. Vosahlo (Equip-
                            ment)

                            Gen. M. Dzur (Rear)

(continued)

## MINISTRY OF DEFENCE

| | |
|---|---|
| Chief of Staff | Gen. O. Rytir (1956-68) |
| Politruk | Gen. V. Prchlik (1956-68) |
| 1st Deputy | Gen. J. Hejna |
| Deputies | Gen. E. Pepich |
| | Gen. A. Gros |
| | Gen. J. Sirucka |

## CZECHOSLOVAK GOVERNMENT
### appointed on 8.4.1968

Prime Minister

O. Cernik

Deputies

P. Colotka

F. Hamouz

G. Husak

O. Sik

L. Strougal

| | |
|---|---|
| Interior: | J. Pavel |
| Foreign Affairs: | J. Hajek |
| Justice: | B. Kucera (Czech Socialist Party) |
| Culture and Information: | M. Galuska |
| Health: | V. Vlcek (People's Czech Party) |
| Education: | V. Kadlec |
| Forests, Water Ec.: | J. Hanus |

(continued)

155

# CZECHOSLOVAK GOVERNMENT

| | |
|---|---|
| Consumer Industries: | B. Machaceva-Dostalova |
| Building: | J. Trokan |
| Mines: | F. Penc |
| Energy: | J. Korcak |
| Agriculture: | J. Boruvka |
| Trade: | O. Pavlovsky |
| Chemical Industries: | S. Razl |
| Heavy Industries: | J. Krejci |
| Defence: | M. Dzur |
| Foreign Trade: | V. Vales |
| Planning Commission: | F. Vlasak |
| Transport: | F. Rehak |
| Technology: | M. Hruskovic |
| Finance: | B. Sucharda |
| Ministers: | V. Hula |
| | M. Stancel |

---

# FEDERAL GOVERNMENT OF CZECHOSLOVAKIA
## appointed on 1.1.1969

### Prime Minister
O. Cernik

### Deputies
P. Colotka
S. Faltan
F. Hamouz
V. Vales

| | |
|---|---|
| Foreign Affairs: | J. Marko |
| Defence: | M. Dzur |
| Interior: | J. Pelnar |
| Planning Commission: | F. Vlasak |
| Finance: | B. Sucharda |
| Foreign Trade: | J. Tabacek |
| Labour: | M. Stancel |
| C. Prices: | J. Typolt |
| C. Technology: | M. Hruskovic |
| C. Industry: | J. Krejci |
| C. Agriculture: | K. Boda |
| C. Transport: | F. Rehak |
| Post, Telecommunications: | M. Smolka |
| C. Press, Information: | J. Havelka |

(continued)

# FEDERAL GOVERNMENT OF CZECHOSLOVAKIA

Ministers:                          B. Kucera (Czech Socialist
                                    Party)

                                    J. Pauly (Czech People's
                                    Party)

State Scer. FA:                     V. Pleskot

State Interior:                     J. Majer

State Plan:                         J. Kraus

State Finance:                      J. Gajdosik (Slovak
                                    Revival Party)

State Foreign Trade:                L. Ubl

State Labour:                       V. Brablcova

---

# FEDERAL GOVERNMENT OF CZECHOSLOVAKIA
## appointed on 9.12.1971

### Prime Minister
L. Strougal

### Deputies
P. Colotka

J. Gregor

F. Hamouz

V. Hula

J. Korcak

(continued)

# FEDERAL GOVERNMENT OF CZECHOSLOVAKIA

### Deputies
K. Laco

M. Lucan

J. Zahradnik

| | |
|---|---|
| Transport: | S. Sutka |
| Finance: | R. Rohlicek |
| Furnaces, Engineering: | J. Simon |
| Defence: | M. Dzur |
| Fuel, Energy: | J. Matusek |
| Labour, Social Security: | M. Stancel |
| Communications: | V. Chalupa |
| Technology and Invest-<br>ment Development: | L. Supka |
| Interior: | R. Kaska |
| Foreign Trade: | A. Barcak |
| Foreign Affairs: | B. Chnoupek |
| Agriculture: | B. Vecera |
| Price Office: | M. Sabolcik |
| People's Control C.: | D. Kolder |
| Minister: | K. Martinka |

1. The chapter is based on Uredni list republiky
Ceskoslovenske, Prague 1945- , Sbirka zakony
a narizeni, Prague 1945- ; and Prirucni
slovnik k dejinam KSC, Prague 1964, 2 vols.

# CHAPTER V

## Judiciary and Security

*The Judiciary*

### Preliminary Remarks

The organisation of the judiciary in Czechoslovakia was inherited from Austria-Hungary. Even
today laws dating back from the 19th century, when
there were two separate national parts, the Czech
provinces and Slovakia and two different legal
systems, are on the Statute book. The Slovak
judiciary was based on the Hungarian model, developed after 1867, while the Czech judicial arrangements were modelled on the Austrian pattern:
district courts on Act 59, 1868, and the system as
such on Act 217, 1896. The Habsburg Monarchy,
which was a Rechtstaat and in Czechoslovakia also
the judiciary, was a separate power which, apart
from administering laws, also acted as arbiter
between the legislative and the executive. Similarly to its functions, its structure was complex and
went back to 1896 (Act No. 217). Two administrative
instructions (Nos. 10 and 81) ordering the internal
organisation and agenda of the courts dated back to
1853. After 1918, only one minor adjustment to the
inherited structures was enacted: a new Supreme
Court had to be established for the Republic (Act
5). (In addition, in 1919, criminal tribunals were
established (Act 451) and in 1932 an administrative
instruction (No. 162) regulated the official
apparel of the judges.) Otherwise all was left
intact. The Constitution of Czechoslovakia, passed
in 1920, took over the Austrian model (paras. 94-
105) almost without any change, while in Slovakia
. the Hungarian judicial arrangements remained in
force. Between 1918-1939, the Czechoslovak
National Assembly passed only two amendments which
affected the judiciary system: in 1923, Act 51,
which created a new State Court, to try security

and anti-state crimes, and in 1928, Act 201, which attempted to harmonise the Czech and Slovak judicial system. Throughout the first republic (1919-1939) this judicial system proved efficient and it was no surprise that the independent Slovak state passed a special law (Act 112) in 1942 which added to the Slovak system features from the Czechoslovak one. During the war, 1939-1945, there was no rule of law in the Czech and ultimately Slovak provinces, and in 1945 Czechoslovakia had to start from scratch and re-build its judiciary. In 1945, the presidential decree, No. 79, resuscitated the old system, i.e. the one that existed on 29 September 1938 (before the Munich Diktat destroyed Czechoslovakia). The Czechoslovak government also dealt with the re-building of the judiciary system in its statement of policies (5 April 1945, Chapter I) in which it proclaimed that it would punish German and Hungarian occupiers and their collaborators. This meant that new courts would have to be created to try such cases.

Some ten types of supreme courts had been in existence in Czechoslovakia before 1948: (i) Supreme Administrative Court in Prague gave judgements in conflicts between the administration and individuals or groups, or between administrations; (ii) the Electoral Court was competent to deal with electoral matters and problems; (iii) the Patent Court; (iv) the Constitutional Court which interpreted the Constitution; (v) the Supreme Court for criminal matters; (vi) the Procuracy General which prosecuted; (vii) the State Court which judged security cases; (viii) the Supreme Finance Court, and (x) the General Military Procuracy which both dealt with military offences by military offenders.

In addition, each province had its supreme provincial court (the Bohemian in Prague, the Moravian in Brno, the Slovak in Bratislava, etc.). These provincial (zemske soudy) courts were subdivided into criminal and civil courts and in Bohemia even into commercial courts. The whole country was covered by district courts in each administrative district and there was a network of

162

regional courts uniting several district courts. The Procuracy's network was on the regional level and it supervised prisons as well. Thus, in 1945 Czechoslovakia reverted to three types of court: (i) civil courts (ordinary, extraordinary and arbitration tribunals); (ii) criminal courts (which could either be jury tribunals or court martial), and (iii) the State Court, as well as the Kmet courts (which dealt with 'public' offences such as libel, etc.). Administrative tribunals such as the Supreme Administrative Court, Constitutional Courts, and the Electoral Courts were also re-established. All judges sitting on these courts were professional men appointed either by the President or the government. The jury tribunals consisted either of 12 men juries and three judges: the jury decided the question of guilt and the judges decided the measure of punishment. However, the reforms effected in 1945 and 1946 defined afresh the powers of the reconstituted courts and, as a result, the post-war system was certainly not identical with the pre-war system.

In 1945, the President issued Decree No. 16 (the Retribution Decree) which created in regional courts the so-called *people's tribunals* which were to try German and Hungarian occupiers and their collaborators. There existed also *people's tribunals* on the district and local levels and they tried cases on these levels. In Slovakia, the Slovak Nation's Council Instruction also established these tribunals and in both cases they were certainly points of departure from the traditional ways of administering justice. These people's tribunals consisted of five to eleven members of whom only the chairman was a professional judge appointed by the President. The four to eleven people's judges were appointed by the government and were selected from the jury lists; on the district or local levels they were appointed by district or local councils on the suggestion of political parties. Occupiers and collaborators of national importance were tried by another special and newly created tribunal, the National Court

163

(Presidential Decree, No. 17). The Slovak
National Court tried the former President of
Slovakia, its government and other collaborating
leaders; the Czech one tried corresponding
collaborators from the Czech provinces. Both
National Courts consisted of seven-men tribunals
whose chairman was invariably a professional judge
appointed by the President, while the 'national'
judges were appointed by the government from the
lists of party politicians who had proportionate
representation on these tribunals. The fact that
the district and local people's tribunals could be
presided over by unqualified citizens and that
'people's' judges at all levels were not jury men
but were instrumental in punishing the accused was
the most important innovation in the Czechoslovak
judicial system. With the simplification of the
procedures at these retribution tribunals,
Czechoslovakia had the first taste of this new
extraordinary justice: many sentences passed in
1945-6 proved extremely severe and only in 1947
did the 'retribution' ardour begin to cool off.
Despite the novelty of the system, after the
Communist coup in February 1948, the Communist
Party decided to destroy it as it was apparently
bourgeois in character.

The systematic destruction of the judiciary
system started immediately after the Communist coup
with the purge of the Ministry of Justice and
courts at all levels. In February 1948, the
minister responsible for this department, Dr. Drtina
tried unsuccessfully to commit suicide, and was
replaced by another lawyer, Dr. Cepicka, who was
Premier Gottwald's son-in-law, as well as an unbal-
anced politician suffering from prolonged imprisonment during World War II in the Nazi concentration
camp of Oswienczyn. Convinced of the utter wicked-
ness of bourgeois justice, Cepicka became the great
destroyer and creator of Socialist justice.

The new Constitution which came into force in
May 1948, already simplified the judicial system
and pointed out the way it would go. It abolished
all but one supreme court; the one left in existence

164

was to judge criminal cases. Obviously the electoral and constitutional courts proved superfluous
for the new system, but the others were to be missed.
The national assembly then passed two acts, No. 319
and 320, which completely 're-organised' the
judiciary. Act 319 'democratised' the judiciary;
only 4.7% of the judges were of working-class origin
and therefore they were all dismissed and replaced
by people's judges, ideologically reliable factory
workers. This was a remedial, immediate measure,
but for the future the Communist Party picked some
3,000 factory workers who were admitted without any
academic qualifications to the Faculty of Law at
Charles University in Prague and in 18 months were
rushed through legal courses which took the qualified students five years to complete. Even while
studying these extraordinary students practised as
professional judges, and on graduation, rather
superfluously, they were appointed to the positions
which they had occupied previously. Act 319 also
contained provisions for the people's judges (again
untrained, hand-picked workers) who joined the
'professional' judges in judging cases. Subsequently
Act 25/1949 fixed the remuneration of these new type
judges and Act 267 put a legal seal on the system.

*Security Organisations in Czechoslovakia 1948-1968*

Introduction

        Prior to the Communist coup d'etat in 1948,
there were two Czechoslovak security organisations:
(i) the State Security (StB) which dealt with
political (subversion, sabotage) security, and (ii)
the HIS section of the General Staff which dealt
with military security (espionnage, counter-
espionnage). Both organisations were formed in
1945 and were under the control of the Ministry of
the Interior and under close scrutiny of the
Ministry of Defence and of the military sector sub-
committees of the Czechoslovak Parliament which
also supervised and checked the activity of the
Ministries themselves. The State Security organisation was headed by A. Zavodsky; General Reicin

was responsible for the military HSIS section.

Before the Communist coup the most notorious case that the State Security uncovered was the "conspiracy against the republic" within the Slovak Democratic Party secretariat in 1947 (Dr. Kempny, Dr. Bugar); the military service scored a success in uncovering the Czechoslovak officers espionnage affair at Most early in 1948. Judicially both affairs remain obscure to this day, for the accused were neither tried nor sentenced in the legal sense, but the political consequences of these cases were far-reaching. Thus the one caused a political reshuffle in the Slovak Board of Commissioners (Sbor poverenikov) as a result of which the Slovak Democratic Party lost its control of that body. The other case caused a crisis within the Czech police force and it became a *cause celebre* by bringing about the February coup d'etat.[1]

It is fair to say that while the Czech Communist Party could easily paralyse the security organisations through its members placed in these bodies, it did not control them and above all could not rely on them to carry out party orders. The Minister of the Interior, Vaclav Nosek, was a veteran Communist who tried hard to control the security services, but his control was far from complete. Moreover, many of the regional and district security departments (which were in charge of security on these levels) were in the hands of non-Communists. In turn non-Communists could paralyse security operations, if ordered by Communist members or the Communist minister. As it happened neither side made use of the security organisations during the coup d'etat, but immediately after it the Communists re-organised the service in order to use it against the defeated non-Communists.

1948-1952

The overwhelming success of the coup d'etat left many Czech Communists astounded. Their opponents simply fled the country or joined them, i.e. became collaborators. It was only in the second half of 1948 that the first attempts at a "come-back" were staged: in July 1948, it was the Sokol (gymnastic) display Festival and in September the funeral of President Be es. These were allegedly the first attempts at a mass counter-coup, and while the Czech Communist leaders were certainly piqued by these demonstrations, they did not take them too seriously. Internally, the Communist leadership felt quite secure despite many successful escapes from the country by non-Communist politicians, army officers and security men (or possibly because of them). However, in June 1948, Jugoslavia was declared deviationist and expelled from the Cominform. At the same time, Gottwald met Stalin in the Crimea and discussed with him the political development in Czechoslovakia. Stalin told Gottwald that he was still far from the complete victory he imagined. Real work would only start now: "with the development of socialism the class struggle would inevitably intensify."

On his return, Gottwald immediately began to take steps to implement Stalin's vague wishes. At first it was thought that Stalin could be appeased by energetic measures and liquidations of the defeated opponents. The new, docile parliament passed the new repressive law, Act No. 213, on 9 August 1948. Sixteen days later Act No. 247 legally established forced labour camps which were to be filled by the purged opponents. The new Minister of Justice, Gottwald's son-in-law, Dr. A. Cepicka, saw to it personally that the tribunals took full advantage of these new laws. Within a month, a whole series of trials was stages; on 2 September 1948 Professor Krajina and his group was tried and liquidated (the Professor, however, succeeded in escaping from Czechoslovakia and now teaches biology in Canada). On 3 September, Captain Blaha and Majors Casek and Nemec were sentenced heavily for endangering the people's democratic regime. Twenty five other officers, among them General Zak, Major Gregor, and Captain Nemecek and Tauchman followed soon after. On 17 September regional

167

courts dealt with their quotas of people's democratic enemies, but there were no death sentences yet.²

In November 1948, the central committee of the Communist Party dealt with Stalin's intensified class struggle suggestions and its conclusion bode ill for the frightened opponents: while in February 1948 they were decisively defeated, now they had to be destroyed whether they still wanted to oppose the Communist Party or not. But for these new tasks the security organisations had to be re-organised for the existing ones could not be trusted. Thus all the non-Communists were purged and either dismissed or imprisoned. Nevertheless, only few specialists were retained while reliable party leaders became district or regional security chiefs. The rank and file of the re-organised services was selected from the workers' militia whose only qualification for the new jobs was a ruthless loyalty to the Communist leadership. The Minister of the Interior lost control of the new body, which now came under the direct supervision of the party praesidium and especially its two leading members, Gottwald and Zapotocky. The re-organisation also put a final stop to any legal basis or control of the security organisations. The ministry and the government as a whole not only lost control over them, but henceforth were not even informed of their activity. Until the creation of the Ministry of Security in 1950, the services were run on a practically private basis by the Chairman of the Czech Communist Party, K. Gottwald, through officials of the central committee and the Politburo secretariat of the Communist Party.

After the coup d'etat many security organisations at all levels were run by ad hoc personnel: at district, regional and central levels, security fives formed themselves, consisting of the 1st Communist Party secretary, security secretary, commander of the security police, commander of the uniformed police and state security administrator. This spontaneous arrangement had many advantages and disadvantages; one of the latter was that it was hierarchically controllable from the central committee. The political element was in control and in a sense guaranteed that the security organs would not run amok. But after the re-organisation only the central five (petka) a purely political and executive body survived; its chairman was R. Slansky, the general secretary and the other members were J. Vesely (executive secret police), K. Svab (political security police), L. Kopriva and A. Cepicka as political representatives.

One of the first acts of the central security five was to abolish the regional and district fives and leave only the security commander in charge. Thus at all levels purely executive officers were left acting on orders from the central five. But the re-organisation also diminished the praesidium's control. Paradoxically it ceased to deal with security matters and only heard reports from the security five. The central five was thus authorised to order arrests, conduct investigations prior to arrests and examine the arrested. Only arrests of important Communist politicians had to be approved by Gottwald and his secretariat. From the beginning Gottwald had an uneasy feeling that the security services could get out of hand. He, therefore, insisted in creating a party body which would have permanent supervision over them and the Control Party Commission was put in charge of security matters and investigations. Though the recommendation was accepted and J. Taussigova became the watchdog of the commission in security matters, this provision proved quite insufficient. Slansky and Kopriva apart from serving on the Central Security Five were also members of the praesidium and only political suicides would dare to investigate or even doubt their word. In 1950 Taussigova dared inopportunely to claim that there existed a Zionist plot in the Carlsbad regional party and was promptly removed from office by Slansky, who as a Jew was the obvious target of this move. Had she waited another year she probably would have been on safe ground. Svab and Cepicka, the other members of Security Five were also in impregnable positions: the former was the brother of M. Svdrermova,

praesidium member, and the latter was Gottwald's
son-in-law. Only the professional, J. Vesely, was
vulnerable and indeed he disappeared without a
trace, undoubtedly after he had done his damage.


## 1949 Arrangement

It is true that while politically the Central
Security Five was well-equipped for its tasks, to
repress the class enemy, professionally it was not
very skilled or experienced. Nonetheless it could
fall back on the old tricks of the trade, i.e.
provocation, forgeries and forced confessions. Old
security experts helped in first few cases. Thus
in May 1949, they used an agent provocateur to
arrest and sentence a "resistance group" consisting
of officers led by General Kutlvasr, hero of the
Prague uprising in 1945.[3] The agent provacateur then
had to be murdered as well. Many similar cases and
the apparent lack of success with "really dangerous
opponents" forced Gottwald to turn to Stalin with
a request for special security advisors. These
specialists were called in not only to help the
Czechs to uncover and liquidate class enemies but
also to catch enemies within the party itself. In
October 1949 two generals of the Soviet Security
Police, Makarov and Likhachev took up their appointments in Prague and shortly afterwards all the
security sections of the Ministry of Security had
Soviet advisors.

It is needless to say that the central
security five was an illegal ad hoc body which somehow formed itself without any proper authority.
However, it was only in 1950 that Gottwald suddenly
decided to "legalise" his security arrangements by
creating a new Ministry of Security. L. Kopriva,
one of the five, became the minister and Svab his
deputy. In the meantime, the security situation
in Czechoslovakia deteriorated to such an extent
that the Soviet advisors began their struggle
against the enemy within the party. Despite

the new Ministry of Security Gottwald continued to
use the special party security commission to
investigate security matters, especially those
concerning party members and party leaders. Thus,
in his party capacity Svab investigated nationalist
conspiracies in Slovakia, while B. Kohler,
J. Frank, A. Baramova and F. Prachar investigated
the Brno affair, which later was turned into an
anti-party conspiracy, in which R. Slansky and
practically everybody in the party leadership concerned with security was implicated.

The repression of the anti-Communist
opposition also continued; during 1950 thousands
of non-communist politicians were arrested and
'passed' through the re-organised security machine.
The results were momentous: in June 1950 after a
show trial the state tribunal sentenced four of the
accused (among them a woman, Dr. Horakova) to death
and many others to centuries of imprisonment.
Significantly politicians of all the non-Communist
parties only were on trial, among them friends of
the ruling party leaders - this was in fact the
first major public trial of the non-Communists.
Many other trials followed, the two most important
ones were those of the Prague and Brno opposition
groups, during which death sentences were pronounced.[4]
Nonetheless these were political trials intended to
intimidate and destroy Communist opponents. So far
no one dared to subject the ruling party to a
purge comparable to that in the USSR in 1937-38 or
1947-48. When the Soviet advisor, Boyarsky,
tried to implicate several leading party members in
the web of investigation of the defeated opponents,
Gottwald put his foot down quite resolutely and had
the advisor recalled to Moscow.

It is probable that the political committee and
Gottwald himself began to realise that the arrests,
investigations, interrogations and public trials of
their opponents would soon extend to the Communist
Party and its leadership and they made an attempt at
stemming this security avalanche. V. Kopriva, the
Minister of Security, later declared that after
attending international Communist conferences on

171

intra-party purges he himself became afraid for his own skin. As an expert he clearly realised that the Soviet advisors and their Czechoslovak helpers were uncontrollable and completely out of hand: for him security work could no longer foster a political career but became a danger to it. In 1951 Gottwald, probably on Kopriva's advice, made the last effort at imposing his will on the security organs and in a surprise move had most of the personnel of the proliferating and illegal apparatus arrested. Svab, Pavel, Bartik, Zavodsky and all the section chiefs for national security were taken into custody as they were leaving a meeting convoked by the polit-buro member, Kopriva. Most of them were massacred and only few survived to tell the tale; one of them, J. Pavel, was destined to play the exalted role of the Minister of the Interior in 1968.[5]

But this massive and bloody purge of the security services failed to solve the ills and dangers of the Czechoslovak Communist Party. Soon Soviet advisors, in particular Generals Makarov and Likhachev, became quite hysterical about subversive elements in the Communist Party itself and aided by such interrogators as A. Prchal, B. Doubek, K. Kostal and V. Kohoutek soon obtained confessions incriminating members of the top party leadership. While persecutions of opponents contin-ued unabated, the security apparatus turned to the party as well and after producing 'proofs' Gottwald and the politburo gave permissions for top arrests.[6]

In fact, the purge of the security organs only provided for its streamlining. The newly appointed security agents were 'specially' selected: most of them had no qualifications for the appoint-ment, but were loyal party members willing to obey orders or fanatical workers militia members. In addition the judiciary was properly purged and new judges and magistrates were appointed. Already in 1948 there was a provision in law 323 that in individual cases judges and magistrates could be appointed without proper educational qualifications. By 1952 the Minister of Justice did not have to have recourse to this provision. In December 1952

225 'special' lawyers graduated from the Faculty of
Law, Prague University. They were all specially
selected Communists without previous educational
qualifications; with brand new degrees they were
prepared to administer revolutionary justice.

Throughout 1952 the party leaders in Czechoslovakia were in a state of excitement. After the
mass arrests in 1951 the purge was snowballing into
a catastrophe and no one knew whose turn it would
be next. Central committee members, ministers,
civil servants, security agents, economists,
generals and intellectuals were slowly pulled in,
each group yielding a given number, as if quotas
had been fixed in advance. Then in November 1952
the greatest political trial was staged in which
the Secretary-General of the Party, R. Slansky,
Foreign Minister V. Clementis and many others were
destroyed. It is true that they all bent the very
law which now liquidated them, but the circumstances
of their demise were so sordid and such a travesty
of justice - the sentences were based on confessions
obtained after torture - that even several party
leaders were appalled. L. Kopriva, Minister of
Security, retired shortly afterwards; in 1968 he
declared that he could not face such terrible
justice, let alone feel responsible for it. He also
added that his own security agents were after his
blood, too.

Throughout 1952-53 the security agents were
busy clearing up the party purges, and while after
Stalin's death the wave of party arrests relented,
this was not because there were no people to be
purged but rather a halt was necessary to clear up
the previous mass arrests. In February 1953 the
most ruthless interrogators Prchal, Doubek, Kostal
and Kohoutek received high decorations for their
performance. Only in 1954 the last of the arrested
in the purges were sentenced (Outrata, Taussigove,
e.g.) and a new look was taken at the security
organisation.

In December 1953 all the satellite countries
were in receipt of a circular letter from the

173

Soviet party leadership in which "Beria and his gang" were blamed for excesses in security services. Czechoslovakia also had a new Minister of Security, R. Barak. On taking over from his predecessor, J. Bacilek, Barak was told that his "machine (Ministry) is simply magnificent; it runs alone and no care is needed; even if the Minister tried to halt it, he would not succeed". However, Barak refused to become such a passive minister; he obviously though that he would build his career on the security machine even if paradoxically this meant destroying it. Nonetheless, it took him almost two years to initiate an investigation of excesses which would lead to the weakening of the dangerous instrument under his control. In January 1955 on A. Novotny's proposal, Barak, Ineman, Kostal, Litera and Svach formed a commission to investigate the abuses of power by the security organs. Shortly afterwards Kostal had to be dismissed, for it transpired that he participated in the very abuses under investigation.

The upshot of this investigation was limited; only a few investigators were dismissed and arrested (Doubek, Kohoutek); the sentences of Smrkovsky, Pavel, Goldstrucker, London and others were revised. On 23 April 1956 the politburo accepted the report of the Commission, but decided to do nothing about it: political upheavels within the Communist orbit were the excuse for inactivity.

After Stalin's death the Czechoslovak Communist Party and its leaders were in a difficult position concerning the security services. To start with it was impossible to take action against them, for they were needed. In June-July 1955 large scale mutinies occurred in the concentration camps in the Jachymov and Pribram areas and the security forces proved invaluable in restoring the situation. These concentration camps were absolutely vital to the national economy, for prisoners worked in uranium mines, and disruption of production would have fatal consequences. In August 1955 hunger strikes and mutinies occurred in one of the largest jails in the country at Leopoldov. Again the

174

security police cracked up this dangerous insurr-
ection. At the same time, however, the party was
quite unwilling to use the security organs against
the party itself: hence the tendency to exclude
security experts at least from factional conflicts
within the party. Thus in 1953 and again in 1956
and 1961, the so-called Yugoslav groups, i.e.
Czechoslovak party members who saw advantages in
the Yugoslav system and advocated its adoption,
were expelled from the party and hunted down in
the social sense - since they were practically all
intellectuals they had to do manual work for tens
of years - but were not arrested, interrogated or
imprisoned. The central committee security
department (Section 8) dealt with these cases,
(Koucky, Pastyrik, Mamula, Kudrna) thus short-
circuiting the security police. But security
police powers still remained wide and in 1957,
when A. Novotny finally became the absolute
leader and Gottwald's successor, he resolutely
refused to curtail them any further, thus making
it clear that he would make use of them if special
circumstances required it.

In 1956, R. Barak, the Minister of the
Interior, headed the 2nd Commission investigating
excesses of the security organs in the party. In
1957 the security policemen who committed crimes
against 'humanity', i.e. crude tortures, were
finally arrested, tried and sentenced to long terms
of imprisonment. However, investigators and even
assassins who practised their crude arts on non-
Communists were either reprimanded and kept on, or
only dismissed from the service: the security
apparat remained intact, apart from notorious
culprits.[8]

The new leader, Novotny, obviously intended
to fall back on this efficient power instrument, if
necessary. Curiously enough he now decided to
use the security police against his own police
chief, Barak, who went round asking embarrassing
questions and reporting to the politburo on past
security mistakes. In September 1958 Barak was
persuaded that no revision of trials during the

175

purges was necessary, but by raising this politically explosive affair he condemned himself. Novotny had this busybody discredited by planting forged evidence on him; he arrested the minister personally and in 1962 had him sentenced to 15 years forced labour.

It is true that in 1963 the party's 'Kolder Commission' rehabilitated the majority of those purged in the 1950s, but it was obvious also that President Novotny was most unwilling to dismantle the security police in a similar way to that of the other Communist countries. He considered it as his personal power instrument to be kept in reserve to be used in any emergency. Thus he continued to protect this agency which carried on its nefarious activity to the last day of the Novotny era. It was allowed to stage several mass trials of non-Communists and party members in the 1960s; the former were usually accused of sedition or subversive activity while the latter were tried for sabotage and subversion. (However, purely political disagreements within the party were usually sorted out by the 8th Section which rarely had recourse to the security police.) In 1967 Novotny tried to intimidate restless intellectuals by permitting the security police to stage another public trial of the writer Benes and of several students for subversion and espionage. To save his own position, in December 1967, Novotny was alleged to have ordered the 8th Section's chief, Mamula, to prepare lists of factional opponents to be arrested. But by this time the very security agents refused to move, because they probably came to realise that they would be blamed and suffer for whatever they would do.

After Novotny's fall in 1968, the security (political) police was finally dismantled and largely dissolved. Curiously enough the Minister of the Interior still remained a 'small' section headed by Lieutenant Colonel Salgovic, Deputy Minister, whose task it was to function as a counter-espionage service. For this purpose the section also retained two Soviet security advisors, Nazorov and Byeloturkin, who were only expelled

176

from the service and the country when the Soviet armies moved to occupy Czechoslovakia in August 1968. Soviet advisors had been in Czechoslovakia since 1949; Barak also had an advisor (Nedvedev), so had his successors Strougal and Kudrna, but these last individuals proved rather obnoxious: they prepared security measures for the invading armies.[9]

In 1968 the security system in Czechoslovakia was thrown into a melting pot and nothing definite has yet emerged. It seems obvious that the security police will never regain its previous power, but if the reform plans and projects in 1968 were carried out, it would be reduced to insignificance. As it is it still exists under the supervision of the Ministry of the Interior, clearly separated from investigation (the Procuracy has been reinstated) and from justice in which sector the Ministry resumed control over prisons; the judges and advocates are given real independence and significance, and the security police is excluded from their domains.

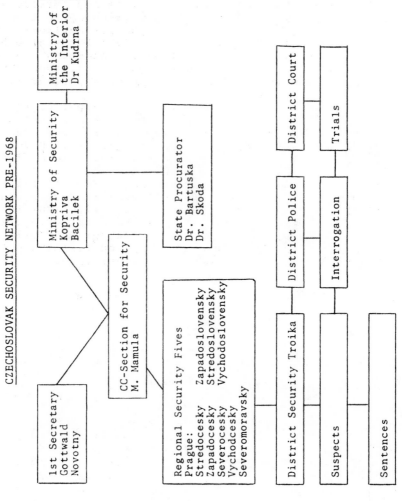

CZECHOSLOVAK SECURITY NETWORK PRE-1968

Ministry of the Interior
Dr Kudrna

Ministry of Security
Kopriva
Bacilek

1st Secretary
Gottwald
Novotny

CC-Section for Security
M. Mamula

State Procurator
Dr. Bartuska
Dr. Skoda

Regional Security Fives
Prague:
Stredocesky    Zapadoslovensky
Zapadocesky    Stredoslovensky
Severocesky    Vychodoslovensky
Vychodcesky
Severomoravsky

District Security Troika

District Police

District Court

Suspects

Interrogation

Trials

Sentences

1.  J. Vesely, Kronika unorovych dnu, Prague, 1959, pp. 43-46.

2.  Ibid, pp. 118-119; cf. also their rehabilitation trial in Svobodne Slovo, 14.2.69.

3.  Svobodne Slovo, 12.12.1968.

4.  Ibid, 17.1.1969.

5.  K. Kaplan, Zamysleni nad politickymi procesy, Nova Mysl, Prague, 1968/6, p 765 ff.

6.  L. Uhlirova, Prokleti moci. Cesta za tajemnstvim Reicinova 5.oddeleni, Hlas revoluce, 10.1.1969, 17.1.1969, 31.1.1969.

7.  V. Brichta, Karlovarsky pripad, Zivot strany, 1968/21, 22, 23; J. Bieberle, Olomoucky pripad, Zivot strany, Prague, 1968/27.

8.  The Czechoslovak Political Trials, 1950-1955, London, 1970, p. 69 ff (Potlacena zprava komise KSC o politickych procesech a rehabilitaci v Ceskoslovensku, Vienna, 1970, which is the original and much better as a source than the English translation).

9.  General Likhachev's death sentence in Pravda, Moscow, 24.12.1954; on Nazarov and Byeloturkin see Rude Pravo, 24.8.1968; cf. also Sedm prazskych dnu 21.- 27.8.68, Historicky ustav CSAV, Prague, 1968, p. 66 ff.

179

# CHAPTER VI

## Dubcek Era

Since Stalin's death in 1953 every Communist Party in Eastern Europe has passed through a crisis: the crises in Poland and Hungary were particularly acute and the Communist regimes were badly shaken in those countries. The notable exception seemed to be Czechoslovakia, where the Stalinist leadership survived the 20th Congress of the Soviet Party and the subsequent de-Stalinisation drive and was forced out of power only in 1968. [

President A. Novotny did not succeed K. Gottwald, the Stalinist leader, directly, but there was an intermediary President, A. Zapotocky, who died in 1957.2 However, Novotny led the party since Gottwald's death in March 1953 and in 1957 he only assumed the presidency of Czechoslovakia, combining the most powerful office of the state with that of the Communist Party.? Though Novotny was a cunning apparatchik who knew how to use the power means left by Gottwald, he was quite unaware of the dangers that threatened him in December 1967: after all he had survived the troubles in 1953, 1956, lived through a whole series of economic crises in the early 1960s and successfully fought off several intra-party bids for a change in the leadership. Thus the minister of the Interior, R. Barak, and his 'group' were arrested, tried and sentenced to fifteen years. Still the factors which brought about Novotny's fall were hardly detectable and even more intelligent party leaders failed to see them. In a sense, Novotny began to prepare his downfall the moment he was forced to head the de-Stalinisation process after 1956. One by one, though extremely slowly his political companions were dropped or dismissed. In 1963, the tough Premier, V. Siroky, went, and the soft J. Lenart, also a Slovak, took over. To Novotny's surprise Lenart seemed a useful, if not reluctant tool, and the President though the government would function as before under

Siroky. At this time, many of the purged Czechs were partially or fully rehabilitated and in 1964 practically all the purged Slovak Communists were similarly brought back into the party and power. Still it seemed that at the 13th Communist Party Congress in June 1966 hardly any changes took place: only O. Cernik replaced another old-timer, Fierlinger, in the party praesidium. But within the Communist Party there were many changes: 43% new members were elected, among them many who had only recently been rehabilitated. Thus it was in 1966 that Novotny had struck at the root of his power, albeit hardly realising it./ After the 13th Congress, Novotny settled down once again to the routine of governing the country: he was convinced that if he continued his slow thaw and pounced resolutely at real troublemakers he could easily maintain himself in power. However, with the introduction of the new economic system and with the recently elected Central Committee buzzing with discontent, Novotny's "old methods" began to fail. If he had continued to play his enemies against each other he might have survived, but instead he proceeded to antagonise even the few friends who were still loyal to him. According to his best friend, secretary J. Hendrych, who also fell, the first secretary hardly ever met the Communist leaders collectively, but instead one by one and he made all the decisions alone.⌐

While Novotny blindly went to his own destruction, three vague factions were formed within the central committee and the Communist Party. The one consisted mainly of party economists headed alternatively by O. Cernik and Professor Sik. Cernik was a member of the party praesidium, headed the Planning Commission and knew full well the precarious state of the Czechoslovak economy, which could not stand much more of President Novotny's ignorant interference. Even though he succeeded in persuading the party praesidium to endorse and introduce the new economic system, he and his fellow technocrats ultimately came to the conclusion that a change in economics should be matched by changes in politics. Professor Sik was the author

of the new system which the Communist Party accepted
after much struggle and in-fighting; he and his
economic experts, politically not so significant
put pressure on the Communist leadership for a freer
hand in implementing their reforms. This 'faction'
was naturally not organised but their discontent
with the present leaders forced them together. Then
there was the Slovak lobby: the latent discontent of
Slovak Communists with Prague centralism was re-
inforced by the rehabilitations of the purged Slovak
Communists. The Slovaks had real grievances,
against the Czech dominated leadership but their
discontent invariably smacked of high treason, and
they could only hope that a change in the party
leadership would bring an equitable solution to
their problems. Necessarily inactive the Slovaks
had been waiting patiently for seventy years for
their chance. The third group was really a loose
collection of the younger Communist leaders who were
rising in the party hierarchy, were critical of the
old generation and despised their "antiquated
methods". These young men had only recently reached
posts of significant influence and they were appalled by the primitive minds and manners of the old
guard. The most experienced among them was D.
Kolder who had joined the praesidium in 1962,
followed by a young Slovak, A. Dubcek, in 1963. It
should be added that this 'generation group' cut
across boundaries and many 'economists' belonged to
it. Several of the key apparatchiki, such as the
regional secretaries in Moravia, Dr. Spacek and
In . Volenik, as well as the Slovak secretary,
V. Bilak, were members. These men saw in the old
men of the 1948 coup d'etat and their compromised
methods of running the country a hindrance to a
bright future. Despite these loose national
groupings Novotny could have stayed in power, had
he maintained the unity of his own faction and had
he not repeated the political errors of the 1950s.[6]

    In 1967, two events took place in Czechoslo-
vakia which administered a coup de grace to the
old leaders. The first was the Writers' Congress
in June 1967; it became the example par excellence
of how not to tackle intellectuals. The

praesidium member, J. Hendrych, failed to cope with
the criticism of the writers and resorted to
bullying: immediately party expulsions followed,
the writers' journal was suppressed and even a show
trial was staged at which a young writer, J. Benes,
was sentenced to five years jail. The events of
the Writers' Congress deeply shocked the entire
party and before it had time to recover the Prague
students who had legitimate grievances, started a
riot and were also suitably repressed. The
students had always been a headache for the old
leaders, as they invariably staged disturbances as
soon as the Communist Party allowed them to let of
steam, usually during May celebrations. However,
in 1967, the repression of student rioting by
brutal police actions had a deep symbolic
significance: the Germans had done it in 1939 and
it seems to have ignited the party revolt against
the Novotny leadership.

Moreover, Novotny was too experienced not to
sense danger from outside the party. In September
1967, when several border incidents occurred and
the guards fired at and killed escapees, he made a
tough speech in which he used the lessons of the
border shooting. The threat misfired as far as the
people were concerned, but frightened his own
faction. The Slovaks, who had apparently been
enjoying equality and autonomy since 1948, began to
voice their demands for new constitutional
arrangements within the Czechoslovak Republic.
Novotny seized on this discontent and in October
1967 during the Central Committee session, attacked
A. Dubcek, a praesidium member and first secretary
of the Slovak Communist Party, for being a Slovak
nationalist. The Slovaks were indignant and only
M. Chudik, the chairman of the Slovak National
Council and praesidium member, supported Novotny
against his fellow Slovaks. All the others,
including the Prime Minister, J. Lenart (also a
Slovak), rejected Novotny's allegations, which in
the not so distant past meant expulsion from the
party and imprisonment. The Slovaks closed their
ranks against the party 'centralists' who became
identified with the Novotny faction and waited for

a pretext to strike at them.

In December 1967, the plenary session of the
Central Committee was to take place and Novotny
wanted to sort out his problems at this session once
and for all: he wanted above all to deal with the
recalcitrant Slovaks. Before the Central Committee
meeting he invited the Soviet first secretary, L.
Brezhnev, to Prague, and thus sought to strengthen
his position. But again he committed some
elementary mistakes.[9] First he allowed Brezhnev to
see the other praesidium members and then permitted
the accused Slovaks to talk to the Soviet leader.
Dubcek who had been educated in the Soviet Union
and spoke perfect Russian, was able to persuade
Brezhnev that he was neither a Slovak 'nationalist'
nor a 'deviationist' and also obtained from him a
promise that the Czechs and the Slovaks would sort
out their problems without Soviet interference.
Thus instead of strengthening his hand, Novotny
prepared his own downfall.[10]

On 19 December 1967 the party praesidium
met to deal with the current political situation
and prepare its recommendations for the Central
Committee Meeting. Novotny and his group failed
to put forward any constructive proposals and forced
together a coalition of Czech 'economists' (Cernik,
Kolder) and Slovak 'nationalists' (Dubcek). Two
of Novotny's friends, J. Dolansky and J. Hendrych,
the latter Novotny's whipping boy at the Writers'
Congress, suddenly and unexpectedly switched sides
and the praesidium reached a deadlock. Novotny
(supported by Lenart, Chudik, Simunek and Lastovicka)
could paralyse the praesidium but could no longer
make decisions. The resolution of the deadlock
now rested with the Central Committee and it was
obvious that it would go against Novotny. It was
therefore in Novotny's interest to adjourn the
plenary session over the Christmas holiday before
any votes were taken and decisions made.[11]

The crisis reached its climax during the
recess. Both sides manoeuvred to strengthen their
positions: Novotny tried to postpone the plenary

session as long as possible, and it only took place after Kolder's ultimatum. Also during the recess, Cernik and his allies learned that according to rumours the President's security man, Mamula, had prepared a list of persons to be arested - the list apparently included Cernik, Dubcek, altogether some 1000 Communist 'radicals'.[12] In addition to this list the President was said to be ready to use the army against the central committee, if it voted against him and his faction. It is almost certain that these were mere rumours but paradoxically they achieved the moral destruction of Novotny. The Central Committee members, who still hesitated, became convinced that President Novotny, whose political past was in any case questionable, was prepared to 'liquidate' them. Before adjourning the December plenary session elected a preparatory commission for the subsequent session and the preparatory commission now voted by 9 to 3 to recommend to the central committee the dismissal of the first secretary.[13]

On 5 January 1968 the central committee met in a plenary session and Novotny himself announced his resignation as first secretary. He remained President of the Republic and tried to have J. Lenart elected as his successor in the party. He obviously aimed at disrupting the unity of the factions against him but failed. His manoeuvres were easily defeated, although the Czech opponents (Cernik, Kolder) did not have it their way either. They had to compromise and Novotny's place was taken by the lonely Slovak outsider, Dubcek. To balance the power within the praesidium definitely in favour of the victorious faction, four new members were added (Spacek, Boruvka, Rigo, a Slovak gypsy and Piller another Czech economist). But the victory of the anti-Novotny radicals within the party leadership seemed tenuous and could easily prove a hollow one, for Novotny still retained his place in the praesidium. Dubcek found out immediately on taking over that Bohemia's capital and five other regions were solidly under the control of Novotny's friends. Dubcek's own Slovakia was hopelessly divided: one region was strictly pro-

185

Novotny (Cvik), Bratislava and the eastern region
firmly pro-Dubcek. The new praesidium member,
Spacek, brought with him to Dubcek's aid the two
Moravian regions (southern and northern) though
the northern (formerly Kolder's fief appeared
undecided. 14

In these circumstances Dubcek had no choice
but to widen the coup de palais and start a
'revolution' from above, first of all in
Slovakia. The Slovak Central Committee met and
resolutely purged the pro-Novotny (ipso facto pro-
Czech) leaders. M. Chudik tried to resign, but
his resignation was not accepted and he was
ignominously dismissed. The pro-Novotny regional
secretary, R. Cⱼik, was also removed and Slovakia
easily submitted to the new leaders. Even
Moravia's quiet adhesion to the new leadership did
not solve the crisis, for the two historical lands
were in a minority compared to Bohemia and the
capital, Prague, which was Novotny's base. At this
stage, Dubcek decided to take the gamble of
appealing to public opinion at large. When late in
January 1968 the journalists of the capital came to
him for the customary guidance and instructions he
told them that they would no longer be guided, but
left free to voice their own opinions and interpretations. Thus he launched a more fundamental
and unusual 'purge' in a Communist country: public
opinion was invoked by the party leadership in order
to take over the party machine. 15

In January 196 it was clear that whatever
came in the wake of the freedom of the press (and
communication media generally) would harm Novotny
more than Dubcek. The radicals were confident on
the whole that they would be able to control the
newly unleashed force: after all they came to the
Central Committee meeting without a plan, were only
vaguely linked together and all the same they had
defeated Novotny and his faction. Now they were
taking initiative and ready for the consequences.
But then suddenly the writers' journal, Litera ni
Listy, and other non-party newspapers launched a
liberalisation campaign of their own. J. Pelikan,

head of the television network, quickly jumped on the bandwagon, while J. Smrkovsky and O. Sik agitated Prague citizens at public meetings and got enormous publicity. The floodgates opened; Novotny and his factionwere made responsible by all accounts for all the past 'deformations' and their nerve cracked up altogether.

On 5 March 1968 it became known that one of the most corrupt and ruthless of Novotny's creatures Major-General Sejna, escapted from Czechoslovakia and defected to the United States. Marshal Yakubovsky had to pay a special visit to Prague to find out the extent of Sejna's betrayal. As far as the Soviets were concerned this defection sealed the fate of the Novotny faction. Dubcek and his friends could purge Bohemia in the usual Communist way without arousing Russian wrath: throughout March 1968 suicides (General Janko, Dr. Brezansky), dismissals and resignations followed each other. Mamula, formerly in charge of the central committee department of Security, had the audacity to call this process White terror. In fact it was the complete collapse of the Novotny faction under the impact of public opinion: however, Dubcek failed to use this out to his full advantage.[16]

Throughout January-April 1968, Novotny and his faction continued to occupy many positions of power; had they kept their nerve Dubcek would have found it extremely difficult to dislodge them. In any case, the new leadership was also split and Dubcek became the leader of a centrist group, while Sik and Smrkovsky headed the radicals. Still, for the moment the two factions united and in order to appease public opinion Dubcek launched two decisive drives against the conservative (Novotny) faction: (i) he decided to draw up a plan of action (the action programme); and (ii) to launch a real rehabilitation campaign to highlight the crimes of the defeated faction. After public discussion the plenary session of the central committee early in April 1968 was to adopt the action programme and sanction a full rehabilitation of all citizens injustly persecuted by the old regime. However,

after announcing its intentions the party leadership practically lost control over the campaigns.
Overnight meetings began to take place at which all
sorts of demands were raised: the workers wanted
increased wages, better management: intellectuals
asked for the freedom to travel (especially abroad),
real elections. Some gatherings even suggested a
new political arrangement and real democracy.
Many of these proposals were to find their way into
the party programme, but a number of them were so
extreme that they had to be rejected by the new
leadership if it were not to renounce power altogether. However, the rehabilitation campaign
finally discredited Novotny and his friends, showing clearly the inhumanity of the old regime.
This time, not only party members were to be rehabilitated, but all the citizens who had suffered
from the legal 'deformations' of the past regime.
The new regime would have to be different, greatly
humanised and much more democratic.

        The pressure of public opinion began finally
to be felt: President Novotny resigned before the
April plenary session of the central committee.
After a spate of regional and district party
conferences, many of his friends were dismissed in
the provinces. Rude Pravo, the party newspaper,
abruptly changed sides on 13 March and the whole of
the public communications system came firmly on the
reformer s side. Dubcek himself made several
radical speeches in which he promise everybody
something: the Slovaks were promised a real federation and all that it implied (additional jobs in
the central government, separate football teams,
local autonomy); the Czechs were offered a free
press, free speech, assembly and association. In
fact everyone could find something to please him
among these promises: they would all come true on
the condition that the 'democratisation' process
did not get out of hand and Dubcek remained where
he was to fulfil them. [17]

        In the meantime Dubcek still had to win the
struggle for the party. After a period of confusion and moral collapse of his opponents, he

convoked a plenary session of the central committee for 3 April 1968. First of all a new praesidium had to be elected: Novotny also resigned from the praesidium before the session and his place was filled by the radical, J. Smrkovsky. It was the turn of Hendrych, Dolansky, Lastovicka and Simunek to resign. Hendrych and Dolansky lost their seats even though they had switched their allegiance to the new leaders in December 1967, when it mattered. Their places were filled with Slovaks and Prague centrists; only Lenart survived though as a candidate member.

The composition of the new praesidium indicated that while the radicals achieved the dismissal of the most conservative leaders, they failed to score a victory themselves: apart from Smrkovsky, Spacek was re-elected and Kriegel newly added. But they lost Boruvka who left the praesidium for the government and Professor Sik was not elected a member. Of the old, only Dubcek, Cernik and Kolder maintained their position, and strengthened it with Prague-Slovak Centrists, Piller, Barbirek, Bi..ak and Rigo. A new praesidium member, O. Svestka, editor of the party newspaper, Rude Pravo, though at the moment lonely and isolated, nevertheless represented the most conservative element in the party. In addition the three candidate members, Lenart, Kapek and M. Vaculik, were keen Novotnyites in the past and their retention confirmed the opinion that the new praesidium was chosen as a compromise solution. The same compromise applied to the secretariat: while J. Lenart represented the old guard, he, nevertheless, counter-balanced the radical member Z. Mlynar, a capable young academic with progressive views. A new secretary, S. Sadovsky, hesitated. As in the praesidum, the radicals (Smrkovsky, Kriegel, Spacek) were checked by the conservatives, leaving the centrists (Cisar, Indra, Kolder) led by Dubcek in control. Thus while the April plenum was undoubtedly a victory for the radical ideas, it was not a victory for the radical faction. During the session Dubcek and his group were forced to listen to the laments and warnings of the old discredited

189

men. Novotny himself was allowed to speak and put
on record that he had always been the most enlight-
ened 'liberal' and that he in fact prepared the
current 'democratisation' process. He was listened
to politely but ignored. It was obvious nonetheless that far from giving up the struggle, the
conservatives were re-grouping. On the one hand,
Dubcek had to appeal for discipline, on the other
hand he had to use the radicals to frighten the
discredited old men. The central committee
approved the action programme, which though vague
contained several concrete points (secret party
elections, right to a passport, etc; division of
executive and legislative power, secret election
with several candidates), which if implemented
would probably have dealt a mortal blow to Dubcek's
opponents and perhaps also to himself.

Subsequently the government still headed by
J. Lenart resigned and a new one was formed by O.
Cernik, leader of the Czech 'economists and
centrists'. The ministers who were going to
implement the party action programme were again
far from radical. The old 'satellite' parties,
the Socialist (Liberal) Party and the People's
(Catholic) Party were treated with the same contempt
as previously and given the old resorts, Ministry
of Justice and Health while all the other
ministries were kept under the direct control of
the Communist Party. It is true that the new
Minister of the Interior was an obscure Communist
veteran, .. Pavel, who during the fifties spent
several months in prison, but this appointment was
more than counterbalanced by the remaining
conservatives, H mouz, Dostalova and Strougal. All
the other departments were more or less reshuffled
and only the centrists strengthened their
positions: the radical Professor Sik was held in
check by Dr. Strougal, former Minister of the
Interior under Novotny who had taken over from
R. Barak when the latter was imprisoned in 1961.

All the party and government changes indicated that a delicate balance of power was
attempted by the centrists. The radical elements

190

either failed outright to gain influence in the party and government, or were suitably kept under control by the old guard. Still as soon as Dubcek achieved this compromise, new pressures arose, and instead of stabilising his position he had to continue his delicate balancing. First the conservatives, who had by now recovered their nerve, tried to stage a comeback. Many of them were re-elected during the district and regional conferences and one, Zourek, even threatened Dubcek and his centrists with the workers' militia. M. Vaculik refused to be a candidate for his old Prague secretaryship, but during the conference which was to elect his successor, delegation after delegation demanded his re-election. In turn, the radicals revived discussions about an official organised opposition party and public opinion swung their way. To eliminate the conservative faction once and for all, pressures were put on the new leadership to convoke an extraordinary congress, elect a new central committee and then implement and institutionalise 'democratic' innovations. Dubcek and his centrists had always been suspicious of these pressures, for in their view they were dangerous and could easily get out of hand. After all, Czechoslovakia was still a member of the Eastern Bloc and any real democratisation would be interpreted by the other Eastern European Communist Parties as a retreat from Communism, and such interpretation could provoke either Soviet or collective Communist intervention in Czechoslovakia. The defeated conservatives used these foreign policy arguments to force the centrists against the radicals whom they represented either as naive or downright 'capitulators'. Thus the first secretary found himself in a difficult position, when with his own faction as yet unorganised he had to get rid of the conservatives and bring under control the radicals. The latter while equally loosely organised had public opinion and communication media behind them and the prospect of Western loans if the internal development went their way. Sooner or later, Dubcek and the centrists had to have a showdown with the other factions if

191

Czechoslovakia was to have political and above all economic stability. The internal solution of the leadership crisis would probably come about at the congress, but the future policies of the victorious faction would have to be an amalgam of ideas and the result of many compromises.[18]

At this stage, no one even thought of solutions imposed from outside Czechoslovakia, albeit the Communist allies, especially the USSR, had tried to influence the Czechoslovak Communist Party from the very beginning of the crisis in 1967. On 23 March 1968 the new leadership of Dubcek was called to Dresden to account for itself: Dubcek       told the five Warsaw Pact allies (Romania did not attend) that the Communist Party had everything under control with the exception of the communications media of whom Dubcek and the new leadership were not afraid. A week later Army General Ludvik Svoboda, a lonely survivor of the post-war era, retired and forgotten, was elected President of the Republic in Novotny's stead. On 18 April 1968 Josef Smrkovsky was elected Speaker of the National Assembly: thus only the party's central committee remained outside the new leadership's control. Later in May 1968 even this 'uncertain' central committee did try to influence events: it expelled from the party Bacilek, David, Kohler, Rais and Siroky, and suspended Novotny's membership and finally convoked the new congress on 9 September 1968 which would finally eliminate the defeated faction, especially from the central committee. Shortly afterwards Literarny listy published an appeal, 2,000 words, which was signed even by some members of the central committee, urging more rapid purges of the Stalinists in public life. Although the appeal received its share of publicity it was not a particularly violent document; however, the Warsaw Pact allies seized on it and were determined to use it to wrest far-reaching concessions from the new leadership. Dubcek, under Soviet pressure, repudiated it: at the same time to demonstrate his independence he refused to attend the Warsaw Pact meeting convoked to Warsaw on 14 July 1968.[19]

It now seems clear that at the Warsaw
meeting (without Romania's participation) the
fate of Dubcek's Czechoslovakia was sealed. The
Warsaw Pact armies, however, did not act
immediately; while the Czechoslovaks continued
to issue appeals galore, the Warsaw Pact command
received permission to send its armies to Czechoslovakia for training purposes: it proved difficult for the new leadership to rid itself of
these allied armies. Then followed the 'last'
attempt at some public resolution of what was now
a dispute between Czechoslovakia and the Warsaw
Pact (Romania being the exception). Late in July
1968, the Czechoslovak and Soviet politbyra met
at Cierna  d Tisou and negotiated the final
modus vivendi made public at Bratislava in the
presence of all the Eastern European Communist
leaders. However, this attempt at accommodation
failed, within three weeks Czechoslovakia was
suddenly occupied by the Warsaw Pact armies and
its crisis more or less resolved.

While up to 21 August 1968, the day when the
Warsaw Pact armies invaded and occupied Czechoslovakia, the problem was whether the Communist
Party could and would remain in power on the
orthodox Stalinist terms, Soviet intervention
transformed this problem into a strictly intra-
party affair. The question now was who within
the Czechoslovak Communist Party would hold power
on Soviet terms. Even with all the naked power
means at their disposal, the Soviets succeeded in
defeating the Dubcek leadership only in April
1969; and then it took two more years to stabilise
the political situation in Czechoslovakia sufficiently to hold a party congress.[20]

It is true that on the very eve of the
Soviet intervention, the praesidium of the
Czechoslovak Communist Party was disunited: the
declaration condemning the invasion was voted by
seven to four (Svestka, Indra, Kolder and Bilak)
but the invasion itself united the party and the

193

nations behind Dubcek, Svoboda, Smrkovsky and Cernik. Profiting from the confusion and the arrest and deportation of leaders the Prague city party organisation decided to proceed with the convocation of the scheduled congress. By 23 August all the Stalinists were eliminated (as well as the 'collaborators') and the newly elected central committee contained only some seven members who would be elected at the 'regular' 14th congress in 1971. The praesidium was immense and contained all the reformers who became prominent since Novotny's fall: A. Dubcek, J. Smrkovsky, O. Cernik, J. Spacek, F. Kriegel, B. Simon, C. Cisar, O. Sik, V. Silhan, O. Slavik, L. Hrdinova, V. Matejicek, B. Kabrna, Z. Hejzlar, J. Litera, E. Goldstucker, B. Vojacek, M. Hubl, V. Simecek, G. Husak, J. Zrak, A. Tazky, S. Sadovsky, P. Colotka, J. Turcek, V. Pavlenda, A. Zamek. However, within a fortnight this 'underground' victory was annulled and the old balance returned: the congress was not officially recognised, the central committee was only supplemented by Dubcek's co-options and the praesidium was as follows: Dubcek, V. Bilak, Cernik, E. Erban, Hrdinova, J. Hettes, Husak, V. Kabrna, Z. Mlynar, K. Neubert, J. Piller, J. Pinkava, S. Sadovsky, V. Slavik, Smrkovsky, L. Svoboda, V. Simecek, Simon, Spacek, Tazky, and Zrak. Still later, in April 1969, most of the reformers were eliminated either by resignation or by expulsion. By then, under the pretext of an anti-Soviet riot in Prague after a victory by CSSR over the USSR in ice hockey, Dubcek resigned and was succeeded by his fellow Slovak, G. Husak. The new first secretary then proceeded with a massive party purge and by 1971 felt strong enough to have himself re-elected as first secretary by a congress.[21]

Though the crisis within the Communist Party and the country lasted over a year, two more years had to be spent on 'stabilisation' or 'normalisation' as the Czechoslovaks called it. This process, in fact, resulted in the return to the status quo ante with one more principle added to the seven basic ones governing a Communist system

in Eastern Europe: this was the principle of
proletarian internationalism denoting clearly
whence it came and the purpose of which was to
justify Soviet intervention in Czechoslovakia.
It is curious to note that Dubcek's reforms
based on the theories of Dr. Mlynar and expressed
publicly in the new party programme of action
meant in fact a return to the situation before
1948 when the then Communist leader, K. Gottwald,
spoke of the Czechoslovak way to Socialism.
Mlynar's theories contained such controversial
proposals as Professor Sik's new economic dynamism (separation of the state and the economy,
market and production) as well as the division of
power, pluralism in politics, 'ethical' Socialism
(with a human face), in which the intellectual
elite would lead (rule), not the Communist Party.
Throughout 1968 these theories had galvanised the
Czech and Slovak nations and they expressed their
approval of these ideas in the only way they knew:
the ideas were made concrete in bills and then
passed by the Czechoslovak National Assembly
(Parliament) as laws.

Although the National Assembly, which on 1
January 1969 became the Federal Assembly, was
composed of the highly unrepresentative members
elected in 1964 (in the scheduled election in 1968
modified electoral laws were to come into force)
its majority still remembered the busy pre-
February 1948 days and the techniques of parliamentary business, so it swiftly adapted itself
to the changed circumstances. While in the period 1964-68 the Assembly met on average in two
plenary sessions a year, during 1968 it held
twelve plenary sessions, some lasting many days.
This meant that parliamentary committees drafting
the bills for the plenary sessions were working
almost without interruption. Thus the January
plenary session approved the budget; in February
the law making Bratislava the capital of Slovakia
was passed. In two sessions in March the
Assembly elected a new President of the Republic,
Ludvik Svoboda, and in April a new Speaker (J.
Smrkovsky) and a new praesidium. During the same

month, the new government's programme was discussed and in May a vote of confidence was given to the new government headed by O. Cernik. In June, a great number of laws were passed: Czechoslovakia became a federal state; the rehabilitation law was passed as well as a new press law; the membership of the new Czech National Council was fixed; the Central People's Control Commission was transformed into a parliamentary investigating committee; work was begun on a new Constitution as well as the government's activity being approved. In July the Assembly elected the new Czech Council and then adjourned for the summer holidays. The committees continued their work throughout the summer even during the invasion by the Warsaw Pact armies. Shortly before the invasion the 26th session was convoked and though it was interrupted by the invasion it passed a whole series of laws governing the federation in September 1968; a new law on the National Front was also passed. In October the plenary session passed a law governing the presence of the Soviet armies in Czechoslovakia as well as the final Federal law, requiring changes in the constitution. Although many laws were not passed (e.g. new electoral law) the extraordinary legislative activity of this 'rump' parliament achieved more than all the parliaments since 1948 and kept the state administration busy supervising at the same time the implementation of its laws.[22]

This new political dynamism found its expression even in the economic sphere in which much less could be done by legislature; moreover the economy had been seriously disturbed by the invasion in August 1968. It was this same dynamism which enabled Czechoslovakia to overcome the economic effects of the invasion. However, in April 1969, the resignation of Dubcek marked the end of this Prague Spring.

196

1. H. Gordon Skilling, Czechoslovakia's Interrupted Revolution, Princeton University Press,
   1976, pp. 3-8, 11 ff.

2. Gottwald had in mind these instructions when
   he told his Central Committee on 9 June 1948
   to stick to the old forms because of their
   international importance (J. Belda, Mocensko-
   politicke zmeny v CSR po unoru 1948, Revue
   dejin socialismu, Prague, 1969/2, p. 234.

3. J. Belda, Ceskoslovenska cesta k socialismu,
   Prispevky k dejinam KSC, Prague, 1967, p. 17.

4. M. Caha, M. Reiman, O nek terych otazhach
   vedouci ulohy strany v obdobi budovani
   socialismu v Ceskoslovensku, Prispevky k
   dejinam KSC, Prague, 1962, p. 860.

5. V. Mencl, F. Ourednik, Jak to bylo v lednu,
   (cont. 2) Zivot strany, 1968/7, pp. 12-13.

6. Ibid (cont. 3) 1968/8, pp. 18-19.

7. W. W. Wallace, Czechoslovakia: Modern History,
   London, 1974, pp. 291-6.

8. Galia Golan, The Czechoslovak Reform Movement,
   Cambridge, 1971, p. 7 ff.

9. T. Szulc, Czechoslovakia Since World War II,
   New York, 1972, pp. 183 ff.

10. Dr. Lubos Kohout, Dokumenty z Barnabitek,
    Kulturni tvorba, 1968/15, p. 3.

11. Pavel Tigrid, Le Printemps de Prague, Paris,
    1968, p. 141-171.

12. Otto Ulc, Politics in Czechoslovakia, San
    Francisco, 1974, p. 65, pp. 111-13.

13. Mencl, Ourednik, op. cit. (cont. 4) pp. 24-
    38.

14. <u>Ibid</u>, (dokonceni), 18 September 1968, p. 12.

15. Radko K. Jansky, <u>The Liberal Stalinist and the Stalinist Liberals</u>, Washington D.C., 1970; also Zdenek Mlynar's book.

16. Skilling, <u>op. cit.</u>, pp. 183 ff.

17. Jan Sejna, <u>Paris Match</u>, 14 August 1971.

18. For all these changes and interpretations, newspapers and their commentaries can be used, in particular <u>Literarni listy</u>. Even after the invasion the central committee began to publish <u>Zpravodaj KSC</u> which remained until December 1969 the most informative source ever published by the Communist Party.

19. For this incredible flowering of Czechoslovak public life cf. <u>Ceskoslovenska federace</u>, vol. 4, Prague, 1969, 89 pp (Spolecenske organizace).

20. Josef Kalvoda, <u>Czechoslovakia's Role in Soviet Strategy</u>, University Press of America, Washington D.C., 1978, esp. 241 ff.

21. For details cf. <u>Sedm prazskych dnu</u>, Prague, 1968 (pouze pro vnitrni potrebu): <u>Tanky proti sjzdu</u>, Vienna, 1970.

22. <u>Tribuna</u>, Prague, 15.1.1969, p. 13.

# CHAPTER VII

## Husak's Federalism

In April 1969, Dr. A. Dubcek resigned and
was succeeded by his fellow Slovak, Dr. Gustav
Husak. It took Husak some eight months in power
finally to condemn his predecessor's plans,
reforms and acts. In November 1969, the Central
Committee issued its Lessons of the Crisis Development and gave instructions for a wholesale retreat..
Under foreign pressure Czechoslovakia re-asserted
all the principles governing a Communist state: it
was a Socialist democracy based on democratic
centralism, collective ownership of means of
production, Socialist legality, the leading role
of the Communist Party, the political system being
the superstructure of the economic system and the
latter regulated by the state plan. This, in fact,
meant the return to the Gottwald and Novotny
system, only with a different team in charge.
After November 1969, the Prague Spring appeared a
waste of time and effort.

Many laws had to be revoked (e.g. the
National Front Act, the Press Act); many were simply not enforced, while the most important one,
the Federation Act, gave the Husak era a semblance
of progress and difference from the Novotny era.
Of course, the application of this law was so
involved and complicated that it did not become
obvious until 1971, what regression Husak's advent
to power meant; even the liberalised electoral
laws of 1967 were discarded by the new leadership;
in security matters it went back to Gottwald and
the 1950s. The newcomer Husak preferred a retour
en arriere even in the top party leadership:   when
after the wild variation of 1968-69, the praesidium
membership was stabilised, only J. Kempny and P.
Colotka remained of those brought up by the mael-
strom of 1968, together with Husak. The rest were
hardliners and Novotnyites: J. Lenart, Novotny's
last Premier; L. Strougal, Novotny's Minister of

the Interior; V. Bilak, Ukrainian Secretary from
Slovakia; A. Indra, the Soviet candidate for
Premier in August 1968; A. Kapek, K. Hoffman and
J. Korcak, all zealous servers of Novotny. President Svoboda, now ailing, remained the only
survivor of 1968, to be eliminated from the
presidency and praesidium through illness and old
age. The division of power among the leading
group was more complicated than under Novotny,
but nevertheless ultimately the same: by 1975, Dr.
Husak became President of Czechoslovakia, thus
once again fusing the top party and state
office into one. Within the party, Husak remained
supreme using the fellow secretaries rather than
sharing power with them: Bilak in international
relations; Kempny in industry; and the rest of the
secretaries being of such junior status as not to
count at all.

To control the party more or less securely
Husak had to purge it severely: he had to eliminate not only his old opponents, the Novotnyites,
but also his erstwhile friends and allies of 1968.
In severity Husak's purge could be compared with
Gottwald's in 1948-49, when he was transforming
the 'democratic' political party into an instrument of totalitarianism. The central apparat of
the party was strengthened and Husak put into it
as heads of central committee departments handpicked Slovaks, making them at the same time
members of the central committee: his private
secretary, M. Beno, entering the central committee
in 1976; V. Bejda in charge of propaganda and
agitation; while M. Kudzej and, after his death,
A. Turzo were controlling military and security
matters; another Slovak, J. Varga, was put in
charge of agriculture. However, Husak's domination of the party was even more complete than
this organisational control illustrates: all the
genuine political leaders had been dismissed as
a result of the upheaval in 1968 and Husak was
really the lonely survivor.

From 1 January 1969, when Czechoslovakia
became a federal republic, new federal institu-

tions came into being, thus enabling Husak to rid
himself of potential rivals in the party; however,
it was only in 1971 that Indra was kicked upstairs
to become the Federal Speaker, while Strougal
became Premier in 1970. After a period of fluid-
ity, Korcak and Colotka became Premiers of the
Czech and Slovak republics respectively and
remained in the party praesidium ex officio both
being 'technocrats' rather than party leaders.
Although the top posts in the Federal government,
and in Czech and Slovak governments, were reserved
for party politicians, the stress was nevertheless
on their technocratic ability: only M. Lucan,
Federal Deputy Premier, seems to be a straight-
forward party hack. The other Deputy Premiers
have either administrative or technocratic back-
grounds, F. Hamouz, V. Hula, R. Rohlicek and J.
Simon. The purely technocratic Deputy Premiers,
K. Laco, J. Gregor, J. Zahradnik are there on their
administrative merit as is the case of the majority
of ministers with the exception of the Minister of
the Interior and Foreign Affairs, who have to be
politicians and are Dr. Husak's choice. Army
General Dzur is another lonely surviver of 1968,
and, despite his being a Slovak, his power has
been declining. The Federal government does not
contain any representatives of the other political
parties, which was not the case in pre-1968 days.

The re-organisation of Parliament also
enabled Husak to displace there the most pro-
Soviet and compromised Novotnyites. The Federal
Assembly now consists of two chambers: the
People's Chamber and the Nation's Chamber. In
addition, each republic has its own legislative
chamber, the Czech and Slovak National Council.
J. Smrkovsky, the National Assembly Speaker, did
not become the Federal Speaker, only the chairman
of the People's Chamber. The Slovak, D. Hanes,
was the Federal Speaker (with a short interruption
in 1969 when P. Colotka and Dubcek occupied that
position for several months). In 1971, after an
election, A. Indra became Speaker; Hanes was
shamefully relegated to the chairmanship of the
Nation's Chamber succeeding another Slovak, V.

Mihalik. J. Marko, until then Foreign Minister, became the first Deputy Speaker, while V. David, Gottwald's and Novotny's Foreign Minister became chairman of the People's Chamber. The National Councils were chaired by E. Erban and O. Klokoc, the least controversial men of 1968. Husak rid himself of all the surviving Stalinists in the Federal Parliament: E. Lastovicka, still very active; V. Novy, much less; O. Volenik, drinking himself ill, while another inebriated Stalinist J. Trojan, killed himself in a car accident. After the November 1971 election, the composition of the Federal Assembly became as arbitrary and contemptuous of the non-Communist parties as under Novotny: while in the Nation's Chamber the Communist Party had 102 seats, the Czech Socialists had 7, the Czech People's Party 8, while the 2 Slovak parties had 2 each. Paradoxically the non-party deputies increased their own representation to 29. In the People's Chamber, the Communists had 143 seats; Czech Socialists 13, the People's Party 8 and the 2 Slovak parties 2 each. Here again the non-party members did well controlling 32 seats.

However, the Federal Assembly after its wide purge in the years 1969-71 lost its significance and became again similar to the Supreme Soviet. In 1974, Vaclav David, Chairman of the People's Chamber, in which federal legislation should be thrashed out and prepared, reported on its activity in the terms of the 14th Communist Party Congress' instructions and central committee resolutions. He called for an improved co-operation with the Slovak and Czech Councils either because these Councils were more active or because they intruded into the federal legislation. Certainly there was room for overlap in the bills prepared and the acts passed: Acts on inventions, and improvements, bills on scientific development, transport and services and especially education and youth whose executive ministries the federation does not possess. Even though David claimed that the committee work was the real basis of business transacted by the People's Chamber, only few important acts were passed between 1971-1974.

Instead, the Federal Assembly seems to have concentrated on foreign affairs (it is, of course, its exclusive right) and on training of its own members to conduct the legislative business in committees and plenary sessions. Thus in the legislature, Husak's normalisation had a deadening effect on the legislative bodies and was, in fact, a return to the 'classical' Gottwald and Novotny days.

It took some time before it became clear how the federal arrangements would work. In 1969, it still looked as if the legislative, executive and the judiciary would be separated and work according to Act 143 passed in 1968. However, the amendments 125 and 43 passed in 1970 and 1971 respectively proved that here there would also be a return to the past arrangements: indeed the 15th Congress of the Communist Party proclaimed its undivided supremacy and made the federation merely responsible for the implementation of its decisions and directives. Although the legislative remained primary on paper, all its powers and prerogatives (control, questions) were amended so that the executive was once again able to work without any control, "according to the Socialist division of labour"; the judiciary likewise maintained Socialist legality. The procedural rules of the Federal Assembly were amended in 1970 (Act 20); the President's Chancellory's powers were trimmed in 1970 (Act 17); rigid federal planning was legalised in 1970 (Act 145), and the acts governing the judges and procuracy were passed in 1969 (Acts 147, 156, 158) and then amended in 1970 (Acts 20, 19).

In the new federal set up, it was not clear how the most important question of state security was resolved. After its collapse in 1968, the security services were taken over by their Soviet counterparts and were only gradually re-established. Albeit J. Pavel, Minister of the Interior, was forced to resign immediately after the Soviet invasion, his veteran successor, J. Pelnar, refused to do much about improving state security whose

203

abuses in the past were the real causes of
Novotny's fall. Dr. Husak had to dismiss Pelnar
and appointed his private secretary, R. Kaska as
Minister of the Interior, before anything was done.
However, already in 1970 the appointment of Major
General M. Kosnar heralded a new era for state
security. Kosnar was an experienced, Soviet
approved security officer, who as a Slovak could
perhaps even be trusted by Dr. Husak. However,
in security matters, Husak had to compromise with
Indra who had his personal secretary, M. Hladik,
appointed as top security operative (in Czechoslovak terms). Hladik, lecturer in journalism at
Prague University, ' ... Doctor of Philosophy,
and former head of the central committee's
propaganda department, is the head of the second
department of the Ministry of the Interior. While
Hladik safeguards the security of the Indra
faction, the security service seems to concentrate
on propaganda actions, such as isolating Czechoslovakia from foreign 'propaganda' and bullying
artists and historians. This security expert,
apart from sentencing a handful of fellow party
leaders for 'anti-constitutional' activities, had
obviously left the responsibility for real security
matters to his Soviet advisers and operatives, who
had installed themselves in Prague in large numbers.
Still to use the security services for even such
limited purposes the Communist Party insisted on
repelling Act 166/1968 in which security matters
were more or less concretised, and superseded it
with a vacuous Act 128/1970. The Czechoslovak
People's Army responsible for external security
was doubly humiliated in the turmoil of 1968: as a
result of Major General Sejna's desertion and
subsequent appeals of Lieutenant General V.
Prchlik for new arrangements within the Warsaw
Pact it was completely isolated within the
alliance; however, with the invasion it failed to
resist and while it might have saved world peace,
it ceased to be an army and to serve its purpose.
Both Dubcek and Husak tried to resuscitate it
(after an extensive and unpublicised purge) by
means of a Council for the Defence of the State.
This Council made some sense while the President

of the Republic and Commander-in-Chief of the armed
forces was a general who was at the same time chairman of the Council, but it ceased to have any
meaning after President Svoboda's retirement in
1975. In any case, the Council since its inception
in 1969 (Act 10/1969) met less and less frequently
until it effaced itself completely on the lines of
the Soviet Supreme Defence Council. In 1969, the
people's army seems to have temporarily found a new
purpose when it was used in August to suppress
popular and widespread demonstrations against the
Soviet occupation of the country. In 1976, at the
15th Congress, the army was finally compensated for,
its collapse in 1968 and its humiliations afterwards by having its representation in the central
party organs more than tripled: in addition to the
Minister of Defence and the Politruk the two first
deputy ministers as well as a vice-minister and
commander of the Western Region were elected. However, the Czechoslovak People's Army still without
a defensive purpose, remains an extremely costly
instrument of power; if permitted by its allies
Czechoslovakia would very much like to cut the
dimension of this useless instrument.

During the year of reforms, it was stated
many times that the independence of the judges and
procurators would have to be guaranteed by law.
However, in the hectic days of 1968 the National
Assembly never found the time to prepare a bill
regulating the independence of courts and procuracy.
Only in 1969 was Chapter VIII of the 1960
Constitution slightly modified, but the constitutional principles governing the courts and the
procuracy were left unchanged. The judges were
'elected', they were 'independent' (without any
other specification), while the procurators were in
charge of the control of 'Socialist legality'. All
these innovations were purely formal, and all that
was really changed were the structures in the terms
of the federation: the Supreme Court of the
Federation and two republican Supreme Courts were
added. Local people's courts were abolished and
their function was taken over by a single magistrate.
The Procuracy was also organised on the federal

level and both republics had their republican
procuracies. The Federal Assembly finalised these
arrangements in 1970 in a series of acts: new
procuracy - modification of Act 60/1965 by Acts
147/1969 and 20/1970; new courts and judges -
modification of Act 36/1964 by Acts 156/1969 and
19/1970. Thus despite new acts nothing was
really reformed in the sector of the judiciary.

'Normalisation' did bring back political
stability to Czechoslovakia. However, to achieve
this Dr. G. Husak, Secretary General of the
Communist Party and President, was forced to return
to the power principles, if not the form of the
demised Novotny and Gottwald systems: practically
nothing was retained of the 1968 reforms. All that
the Husak system has to show for its arbitrariness
and lack of freedom is qualified economic success.
However, even under Gottwald and Novotny the
Czechs themselves used to joke about the lack of
aspiration for greater freedom provided the people
had 'enough beer and pork and dumplings with
sauerkraut'. Still 1968 has proved this to be a
hollow joke and if sometime  in the future Dr.
Husak decides to liberalise his system he may find
himself in the unique position of actually asking
his Soviet ally to re-intervene on his behalf in
Czechoslovakia.

# APPENDIX I

## Note on Czechoslovak Security and Foreign Policy

Early in 1945, when the foundations of Czechoslovakia's internal and external security were
laid, they were entirely based on foreign policy
factors. The country itself was occupied by the
German and Soviet armies; its government and
parliament were in England and Soviet Russia,
where there were also standing armies which fought
in the war. President Benes was trying to shape
the post-war development in the power vacuum of
exile, largely through international politics.
In this sphere President Benes proved himself to
be a past master at power balancing acts. Against
all international odds, Dr Benes had himself
recognised as the legal representative of Czechoslovakia in exile; initially by Britain and
France and in 1941 by the USSR. Subsequently
Dr Benes used the USSR power card so skilfully
that he forced his erstwhile allies and guarantors
even to repudiate the Munich agreement as null and
void, and to gain recognition and concessions even
from the United States.[1]

Before his departure to Czechoslovakia via
Moscow, President Benes scored his last success in
Britain. While he and his army were totally
dependent on the British, whose political aims had
to be respected, Benes, by using the Soviet card,
decided to defy the British and to transfer the
Czechoslovak Germans to the Reich at any price and
whatever the internal political consequences.
Premier Churchill and Foreign Secretary Eden told
Benes that Stalin, at the Yalta conference, refused
to deal with this matter, but Benes answered that
once in Moscow, he would deal directly with Stalin
and sort out the problem without the Western
allies, whom he suspected of dragging their feet,
if not blocking this Czech idea of solving their
nationality problem once and for all.[2] In order
to achieve this, Benes was ready for any political
sacrifice, even subordinating Czechoslovakia's

207

foreign policy to Stalin's

On 24 February 1945, President Benes had a
farewell dinner with Premier Churchill at Chequers.
Churchill warned Benes not to become too dependent
on the Soviet Union and made it clear that Britain
and the United States could not guarantee Czechoslovak sovereignty vis-à-vis the USSR.    If the
USSR went too far, Britain and the US would resist
it, but they would not be able to stop Soviet
expansion except on the Channel.    After telling
Benes such unpalatable truth, Churchill reiterated
his previous advice on the German problem:  do not
transfer the population until you have Allied
consent.[3]    Once again Benes was under the
impression that Churchill did not favour the
transfer of the German population to the Reich and
became convinced that he would have to get it from
Stalin at whatever price.    Thus even before Benes
had left for Moscow, he was burning his bridges
with the West (meaning Britain because the USA
were simply not interested in European problems)
and putting himself completely in Stalin's power.
Subsequently Benes had to pay the price and concede
three fundamental points:  he had to agree to
Stalin's demands concerning Ruthenia;  to the
Czechoslovak Communist Party's power position in
the future political system, and the Czechoslovak
army's role in the post-war period.    It would be
too simple perhaps to claim that President Benes
did not realise the risks that he was taking but
nonetheless he could not have appreciated them
then as fully as we can with hindsight.    Still,
in 1945 he convinced himself and the West that,
while he was in power, he could handle the
'siutation' and solve further problems in his (and
Czechoslovakia's) favour.    Thus the country's
internal and external security depended almost
exclusively on the President.    Very soon after
Benes had put himself into Stalin's hand, warning
signs began to multiply showing that his moves
were unwise.

Stalin resolved the Ruthenian problem abruptly
and the Provisional National Assembly (Parliament)

ceded the province to the USSR on 29 May 1945,
roughly thirty years after it had be acquired.
Albeit "many grievances were aired and doubts
about the Czechoslovak dependence on the USSR
proved widespread", the Communist Party dominated
the debate and the final decision to give up
Czechoslovak territory was unanimous.[4]  As for
the power position of the Czechoslovak Communists,
Benes negotiated it on the spot in Moscow before
leaving for Czechoslovakia.  According to the
British annual report on Czechoslovakia, Benes
made unreasonable concessions to the Communist
Party in order to get Stalin's backing in international affairs:  although the government
consisted of ministers representing equally the
four permitted Czech parties (with two Slovak
parties), the Communists secured for themselves
all the key positions, in particular the Ministry
of the Interior.  However, the British still
thought that President Benes did not surrender
power to the Communists, for he had kept the
Ministry of Defence, which meant the army in the
field, under his and General Ludvik Svoboda's
control.  It was thought that Svoboda, in command
of the Czechoslovak armed forces in the USSR, who
was a non-party 'expert', would be loyal to the
President, who appointed him as Minister of
Defence, although Svoboda was in sharp conflict
with the London military leaders.  Dr Benes
resolved the Svoboda-Ingr dispute in the former's
favour, but this cost the President dear; as a
result he virtually lost control over the armies.
In fact it now appears evident that the Czechoslovak post-war system had no armed forces to
secure it in case of need, from the very beginning.
General Svoboda, who was a secret Communist as we
know now with certainty, on being appointed Minister
of Defence launched a 'purge' of the armed forces
as early as 25 April 1945.  He took over command
from General S. Ingr and immediately replaced
B. Miroslav (Neuman) as Chief-of-Staff by General
B. Bocek.  General Fr. Moravec, head of Intelligence, was also removed and all three generals were
suspended and put on full-pay leave.  President
Benes must have been disturbed by these moves,
because in August 1945 he sent a letter to his Prime

Minister, Fierlinger, pleading their reinstatement.
However, Benes's intervention served no purpose;
General Svoboda formed a Military Council attached
to the Premier's office, which in effect excluded
President Benes (who remained supreme military
commander in name only), from all the military
decisions.5    In June 1945, General Svoboda further
increased Communist influence in the armed forces
by forming the Main Administration for Education
and Enlightenment which was headed by his deputy,
Dr Prochazka, member of the CP central committee.6
Thus, Benes, though nominally Commander-in-Chief,
no longer controlled the army, the only power means
that he had left after the war, for the police was
firmly under the control of the Minister of the
Interior, V. Nosek, another Communist.    While in
1945 it was evident to all except the United States
that Czechoslovakia had become a Soviet satellite
in foreign affairs, the West continued to cherish
the illusion that President Benes at least
controlled the internal security of the country,
right up to February 1948.    In fact internally
he was dependent on the agents of the USSR, and
could maintain internal autonomy only as long as
they (the Czechoslovak Communist Party) permitted
him.    Thus the post-war political system in
Czechoslovakia rested on most unstable foundations:
in reality the Soviet Union and its agents
basically controlled both the internal and
external affairs of Czechoslovakia and it was
only a question of time and opportunity before
they took over openly.

Both Western allies based their attitudes to
Czechoslovakia on faulty premises.    While the
British considered that the country's security was
safeguarded as long as President Benes remained in
power (largely due to their belief that he
controlled the armed forces), the Americans were
convinced from the very beginning that the country
was run by socialists and communists and therefore
refused to aid Czechoslovakia economically and lend
support to the non-Communists.7    Both the British
and the Americans were shocked by the wholesale
nationalisation of industry in October 1945, and
while the British did nothing, the Americans became

openly hostile: they wrote off Czechoslovakia as
a full Soviet satellite. Their Ambassador,
Steinhardt, who should have known better, only
abandoned his hostility in December 1947, when it
was too late to do anything practical such as
aiding the non-Communists: by then Gottwald's
Communist Party was ready and determined to carry
out a coup d'état.[8] Paradoxically though, the
Americans were uninterested in Czechoslovakia;
they were better informed, in particular about the
impending coup d'état, than the British. The
State Department had a detailed report as early as
13 December 1947.[9] Richard Reinfuss informed
Ambassador Steinhardt that a putsch similar to that
in Hungary should be expected shortly in Czechoslovakia. It is possible that Reinfuss obtained
this information from the Brno regional secretary,
O. Sling, who was undoubtedly in the know as a
member of the central committee. However, the
revelation of the fact was not so important as the
manner in which the putsch would be carried out.
(The British also suspected that a coup d'état
would take place - in fact they thought something
was afoot in June 1947 when Vyshinsky, Marshal
Koniev and twenty other prominent Russians were
taking the waters at Carlsbad.[10]) According to
Reinfuss, the Russians (he meant their agents)
were increasing control in the Czechoslovak armed
forces - in view of the currently widespread
arrests of army officers who had served in the
West this seemed a most valid point even to the
State Department official who had minuted this
report.[11] At the same time a bitter propaganda
campaign was launched against the United States
accusing it of being fascist and pro-German.
Both these moves were obviously aimed at
neutralising the armed forces when the coup was
launched. To neutralise the army still further
and also to break political morale in Czechoslovakia, the Soviets were going to move train-
loads of troops, tanks, guns and vehicles from
the Ukraine towards Czechoslovakia and Austria.
The State Department passed the report to the
Foreign Office and both brushed it aside as
inaccurate: the situation in Czechoslovakia was

not the same as in Hungary. Nonetheless the
Western allies never even bothered to warn
President Benes, and within two months the report
proved correct. By depriving Benes and Czechoslovakia of the control of its armed forces,
Stalin and the Soviets made sure, as early as
1945, that an open takeover in the form of a
Communist putsch would not end in a protracted and
bloody civil war. Moreover, by offering the
Czechoslovak Communists 'moral support' through
external pressure, such as troop movements, and
with the West remaining uninterested and passive,
the Soviets made sure that the weak Czechoslovak
politicians and the demoralised people gave up
even the thought of resistance against such overwhelming odds.[12]

It appears that these external factors were
of paramount importance to the success of the
Communist putsch; however, internal factors were
of great importance for the coup itself. Although
the West was unprepared to do anything for Czechoslovakia in international affairs, such as to
offer counter pressure, especially since it knew
of the Soviet and Communist intentions, it nevertheless considered it right that the liberal
democratic system should continue there. However,
instead of underpinning it with economic aid and
possibly with political gestures, it continued to
rely solely on President Benes to uphold the
Czechoslovak system. Both sides were guilty of
misjudgements. Throughout 1945-57, Benes rather
complacently kept assuring the West that he could
cope with the situation. Curiously enough, Benes
was rather pleased when in 1946, after the general
election, he dismissed the Social Democratic
Premier, Z. Fierlinger, whom he distrusted, and
replaced him by the Communist leader, K. Gottwald.
He evidently underestimated the 'simple alcoholic'
carpenter and instead concentrated his political
ire on the 'sinister' Slansky, who "would cause
real trouble if it ever came to a conflict".[13]   It
is now well documented that in 1947, when Dr Benes
made his comments on his liking Premier Gottwald
who had a slight drink problem, the latter was
firmly in charge of the preparation of a coup.[14]

In addition, Dr Benes viewed his own position vis-a-vis the army and the secret police unrealistically. On his sixty-third birthday Benes let it be known all round, even as far away as London, that he would be shortly curbing the illegal doings of the secret police (StB) and ridding the armed forces of Communist influence.[15] This was possibly the greatest error in Benes's life, and in mitigation it should be stressed that he was gravely ill. Almost as if in response to this strong statement, the secret police made its omnipotence clear to everyone: far from being curbed, it was rehearsing in Slovakia the planned coup for the whole country. When on 5 December 1947 Ambassador Nichols reported to the Foreign Office his farewell dinner with President Benes, he made it clear that the President was an ill and broken man; he added that his disappearance might be a catastrophe for Czechoslovakia.[16]

The other misjudgement of President Benes which ensured that a Communist coup would be successful, was his hostility towards and neglect of Slovakia and Slovak non-Communist politicians. It became quite clear, after the election in May 1946, that Slovakia with its non-Communist majority, would be a key to the internal balance of power and it was therefore in the interest of President Benes and internally independent Czechoslovakia that the Slovak Democrats, who had scored such a victory in the election (they obtained forty-three seats as compared to the Slovak Communists' twenty-one seats) co-operated with and allied themselves closely with Czech non-Communists. Though initially Dr Benes was favourably disposed towards the Slovaks, he was shocked at Kosice in 1945 by the measure of autonomy which the Slovaks had obtained for their province with Communist support. Now after the election in 1946, which they badly lost in Slovakia, the Czechoslovak Communists appeared willing to curtail 'non-Communist Slovak autonomy' and after attacks on the Slovak Democrats in the Prague press, they did indeed reduce the authority of the Slovak National Council on 18 June 1946.[17] With President Benes's approval, the Communists pressed on with their attacks on Slovakia. After the summer holiday,

213

between September and December 1946, they conducted a vicious campaign of denigration against the Slovak Democrats, especially when the latter decided to seek political support in the United States. The Slovak Democrats, a new party, were an amalgam of Christian Democratic forces which became united after an agreement signed on 30 March 1946 which brought it electoral success. Paradoxically, while the Communists were attacking the Slovak Democrats as being reactionary, the Czech non-Communist parties were disturbed by the Slovak political moves in the United States, where there is a sizeable Slovak minority. The spectrum of Slovak separation still haunted Benes and the Czech non-Communists. As a result, Czech-Slovak relations were rapidly deteriorating and that enabled the Slovak Communists to turn gradually the electoral defeat into a victory over the Slovak Democrats: first of all, they intimidated them with their influence in the Czech provinces and especially in Prague, where the Communist leader was Prime Minister; on the spot they used quite brutal intimidation - they spread rumours that in a crisis they would ask the Red Army to help them defeat the Slovak Democrats; and to curtail Slovak autonomy even further, the Slovak Communists took over Czech chauvinist slogans telling the Slovak Democrats that they would have "as much autonomy as they could afford to pay for".[18]

In the first half of 1947 the situation in Slovakia became even more tense with rumours of another war between the USSR and USA. President Benes warned the Slovaks solemnly not to break up the Czechoslovak republic, while Premier Gottwald attacked the Slovak Democrats as a disloyal opposition and likened them to the pre-war Hlinka party. This concentrated campaign against the Slovaks was obviously a Communist ploy, but the Czech non-Communists joined in willingly, because of their unrealistic fears of Slovak separatism. According to the British reports from the province, the Hlinka (separatist) followers were no longer dangerous; it was Slovak disunity, flaccid political leadership that constituted real danger;

214

journalism was apparently spineless and Slovak
economic planning chaotic; labour shortage was
widespread because of the transfer of Slovaks to
Bohemia and Moravia to replace expelled Germans.[19]
President Benes was told of this British
appreciation, but he nevertheless continued in
his hostile attitudes towards the Slovaks, though
it made no political sense and in fact endangered
the non-Communist cause. Early in 1947 the former
President of Slovakia, Msgr. Tiso, stood trial for
collaboration with Germany and treason against
Czechoslovakia. As expected, the National Court
sentenced him to death, but it was also widely
expected that President Benes would pardon him and
commute the death sentence. When the case was
referred to Prague, the Czechoslovak government
upheld the sentence by 16 votes to 7 (Slovak
Democrats and Catholic (People's) party ministers
dissenting); President Benes therefore confirmed
the sentence and Msgr. Tiso was hanged at five
o'clock in the morning of 18 May 1947.[20] After
the execution the Slovak mood became sombre and
solidly anti-Czech, so much so that it prompted
the British Embassy to send a fact-finding mission
to Slovakia.

On 13 October 1947 Mr (later Sir) Cecil
Parrott despatched to London his findings which
sounded really alarming: the situation in
Slovakia was more critical than was thought.
After the events in Hungary (where the Communists,
with the help of the Red Army, had taken over)
Slovak Democrats became convinced that the Slovak
Communists would imitate their Hungarian comrades
in Slovakia. After all, they were defenceless
for the police was under the Ministry of the
Interior in Prague, which was under Communist
control. The former Hlinka guards (a paramilitary
militia) had apparently joined en masse the
Communist party and the Slovak Democrats had no
power instrument at their disposal. For reasons
of balance of power, Mr Parrott urged the British
government to help Slovakia politically; the
British should do their best to encourage the
Slovak Democrats in their resistance to the Slovak
Communists; they should be reconciled with the

215

Czech non-Communist parties; and more contacts should be established between Britain and Slovakia.[21]  Although the Consul General, A. J. Grant, supported Mr Parrott's report and recommendations without reservations, the British government was not interested in playing a power game in Slovakia, nor in saving Czechoslovakia from possible disintegration.  Neither, it seems, were the Slovaks themselves interested in British support.[22]  By now all the Slovak politicians knew full well that if the Soviet Consul-General in Bratislava supported openly the Slovak Communists, Slovak Democrats were in need of support, not from the British, but the American Consul General, and the Americans consistently refused to play this game.  While the Slovaks realised that even if the USA were willing to enter the balancing game against the USSR, it would protect them as long as the two superpowers did not actually draw a clear line between their 'zones of influence' (according to this reasoning, Czechoslovakia was at this moment in a grey zone). But in any case the British government refused to back its diplomats and the Slovaks were left to their own devices.

On 14 October 1947, Mr Grant reported from Bratislava that the Communists finally found a pretext for the suppression of the Slovak Democrats.  Vice-Premier Ursiny's office was raided by the secret police (StB) and it was established that his private secretary, Otto Obouch, had been sending confidential Cabinet papers to Dr Datelinka, a Slovak separatist living in Stockholm.  Two Catholic secretaries of the Democratic Party, Dr Kempny and Dr Bugar, were implicated in this affair;  they were dismissed from their posts and arrested.  As a result widespread arrests followed, operated by the Prague secret police under Captain Pokorny.  The Slovak Ministry of the Interior, under General Ferjencik (a Democrat), was being kept out of this case.[23]  On 20 November 1947, Mr Parrott finally warned the Foreign Office that the Slovak crisis had reached its peak and that nobody by now could help the Slovak Democrats.  On 17 November 1947,

A. J. Sington reported that the Democrats were
decisively weakened and that Dr Lettrich, their
leader, was certainly less powerful than Dr Husak,
the Communist leader.[24]  In fact the Communists
had rehearsed a coup procedure and found out that
it had worked well in Slovakia;  they could proceed
to organise a national coup.

The defeat of the Slovak Democrats in their
own province was tacitly tolerated by almost all
the Czech politicians who, instead of closing their
ranks in the face of Communist danger, continued
disunited and hostile as ever towards the Slovaks
and each other.  As far back as 1946, President
Benes complained about the flabby leadership of
the Catholic (People's) Party and its non-
co-operation with the Liberal (National Socialist)
Party.  It was only after the Slovak crisis in
December 1947 that disputes between the two Czech
parties stopped and the two leaders, Msgr, Sramek
and Dr Zenkl, began to speak to each other and
co-operate.[25]  The Social Democratic Party was
divided into three factions and a leadership
struggle was resolved rather inconclusively in the
autumn of 1947:  Fierlinger's left-wing was
defeated, but the right-wing led by V. Majer,
which won the battle, was outmanoeuvred by the
centrists, led by B. Lausman, who became party
chairman, so that no one seems to have led the
party.  This confusion within the Czech Social
Democratic Party made co-operation with other Czech
parties impossible, as was subsequently demonstrated
during the Communist coup in February 1948 when
the Social Democratic ministers (with the exception
of Majer) failed to resign from the Gottwald
government and so kept it in power.[26]  This
unsatisfactory state of affairs was widely known
and a Communist takeover was expected at any time.
The departing British ambassador warned both his
government and President Benes that the Iron
Curtain would come down on Czechoslovakia within
a year and the Communists would take over power
openly.  However, nothing could really be done by
Great Britain to prevent the takeover, as the
United States refused to get involved.[27]  Two
months before the coup d'état, on 13 December 1947,

217

V. Kudratsev wrote openly in the Izvestiya that Czechoslovakia was no longer a bridge between the East and the West.  It no longer sat on the fence: it warded off American monopolistic enticement in the Marshall Plan and Soviet unselfish economic aid made it a member of the Eastern bloc.[28]  There was no Western reply to this claim and the Czechoslovak Communists seem to have been given the final go-ahead with the takeover, which was on the cards ever since 1945, when President Benes made his fundamental political misjudgements: accepting Stalin's sponsorship in international politics;  underestimating the Czechoslovak Communist leaders;  overestimating the non-Communist leaders, and maintaining political hostility towards the Slovaks.

On the other hand, these British documents show clearly that the war-time allies, the United States and Great Britain, were sticking tacitly to the hegemony arrangements worked out in the last phase of the war largely by President Roosevelt and Premier Churchill.  It appears that despite American interests in Poland and Czechoslovakia, Britain held diplomatic sway over Europe and those two particular Eastern European countries.  But since the British Labour government refused to be involved in the power struggle with the USSR especially in Eastern Europe, it appears that in fact the area was abandoned to the Russians ever since the end of World War II.

1. L. Otahalova, M. Cervinkova (eds.), Dokumenty z historie ceskoslovenske POLITIKY 1939-1943, Vol. 1, Prague, 1966, pp. 15-414; Vol. 2, 23 July 1941, Benes to Eden; 4 June 1942, Benes to Fierlinger; 2 September 1942, Churchill to Benes; 21 June 1943, Smutny to Benes (minutes of his talk with A. Ye. Bogomolov).

2. Ibid., p. 749, 13 February 1945, Benes to Nichols.

3. Ibid., p. 750, 24 Feburary 1945, Benes to Churchill.

4. Public Record Office, London: Foreign Office (hereafter abbreviated FO) 371/56085 Annual Political Review for 1945.

5. FO 371/47124 Czech Intelligence Summary, 25 April 1945; also Dokumenty . . ., op. cit, pp. 751-54, 1 August 1945, Benes to Stransky; August 1945, Benes to Fierlinger.

6 M. Lichnovsky, O Nekterych otazkach zmeny v tempu budovani CSLA v letch, 1. petiletky, Historie a vojenstvi, Prague, 1966/2; cf. also J. Navratil, J. Domanksy, Boj KSC o lidovou armadu 1945-1948, Prague, 1963.

7. FO 817/57, 8 November 1947, Nichols to Bevin; the Americans, for example, suspended $40 million of the $50 million credit given to Czechoslovakia to purchase surplus war goods, and at the same time negotiations for a $50 million loan from the IMF were suspended, too. Secretary of State, J. F. Byrnes, took this decision in Paris in October 1946, after he had observed that Foreign Minister Jan Masaryk consistently voted with Molotov at the peace conference.

8. FO 817/57, 11 December 1947, Nichols to Bevin; L. A. Steinhardt's papers are in the Library of Congress, where they can be consulted.

9.   FO 371/65787 Top Secret US CX, 13 December 1947.

10.  FO 817/49, 2 June 1947, Hankey to Nichols.

11.  FO 817/57 Political Arrests, 14 November 1947, Parrott to Rumbelow.

12.  P. Tigrid, 'The Prague Coup of 1948', The Anatomy of Communist Takeovers, Yale, 1975, pp. 399-432; cf. also his comments on the coup in Svedectvi, Paris, 1977.

13.  FO 371/65785, 12 September 1947, Nichols to Bevin.

14.  Revue dejin socialismu, Prague, 1968, pp. 227-250.

15.  FO 371/65784, 4 June 1947.

16.  FO 371/65787, 5 December 1947, Nichols to Hankey, Secret.

17.  FO 371/65784 Annual Political Review for 1946.

18.  FO 371/65784 Political situation in Czechoslovakia, September-December 1946.

19.  FO 817/56, Grant to Nichols, 30 July 1947.

20.  FO 817/49, 8 May 1947, Nichols to Bevin.

21.  FO 817/46, 13 October 1947, Parrott to Bevin.

22.  FO 817/46, 15 Octover 1947, Grant report.

23.  FO 817/46, 14 October 1947, Grant to Nichols.

24.  FO 817/46, 17 December 1947, Sington to Parrott.

25.  FO 817/56, 20 November 1947, Parrott to Rumbold.

26.  FO 371/65785, 25 June 1947, Nichols to Bevin;

29 August 1947, Hankey to Rumbold.

27.  FO 371/65787, 17 December 1947, Nichols to Bevin.

28.  FO 817/49, 13 December 1947, Moscow Embassy to Foreign Office.

# SELECTED BIBLIOGRAPHY

E. Benes, Memoirs of Dr Eduard Benes, Boston, 1971

L. Bittman, The Deception Game, Syracuse, 1972

J. F. N. Bradley, Czechoslovakia: A Short History, Edinburgh, 1971

V. Busek & N. Spulber (eds), Czechoslovakia, New York, 1957

E. J. Czerwinski & J. Piekalkiewicz (eds), The Soviet Invasion of Czechoslovakia: Its Effects on Eastern Europe, New York, 1972

I. Duhacek, The Strategy of Communist Infiltration: The Case of Czechoslovakia, New Haven, 1949

Paul Ello, Czechoslovakia's Blueprint for 'Freedom', Washington DC, 1968

G. R. Fiewel, New Economic Patterns in Czechoslovakia, New York, 1968

J. Frolik, The Frolik Defection, London, 1975

K. Glaser, Czecho-Slovakia: A Critical History, Idaho, 1961

G. Golan, The Czechoslovak Reform Movement, Cambridge, 1971

_____, Reform Rule in Czechoslovakia, Cambridge, 1973

D. Hamsik, Writers Against Rulers, London, 1971

R. R. James (ed.), The Czechoslovak Crisis, London, 1969

B. Jancar, Czechoslovakia and the Absolute Monopoly of Power, New York, 1971

R. K. Jansky, The Liberal Stalinist and the Stalinist Liberals, Washington, 1970

J. Kalvoda, Czechoslovakia's Role in Soviet Strategy, Washington, 1978

J. Kirschbaum, Slovakia: Nation at the Crossroads of Central Europe, New York, 1960

J. Korbel, The Communist Subversion of Czechoslovakia, Princeton, 1959

V. V. Kusin, The Intellectual Origins of the Prague Spring, Cambridge, 1971

_____, Political Groupings in the Czechoslovak Reform Movement, London, 1972

_____, From Dubcek to Charter 77, Edinburgh, 1978

J. Lettrich, History of Modern Slovakia, New York, 1959

Robert Littell, The Czech Black Book, New York, 1969

E. Loebl, Sentenced and Tried, London, 1969

A. London, On Trial, London, 1968

R. Luza, The Transfer of the Sudetan Germans, A Study of Czech-German Relations 1933-1962, London, 1964

V. S. Mamatey & R. Luza, A History of the Czechoslovak Republic, 1918-1946, Princeton, 1973

V. Mastny (ed.), Czechoslovakia: Crisis in World Communism, New York, 1972

J. A. Mikus, Slovakia: A Political History, 1918-1950, Milwaukee, 1963

B. B. Page, The Czechoslovak Reform Movement, 1963-68, Amsterdam, 1973

J. Pelikan, The Czechoslovak Political Trials,
London, 1971

_____, Socialist Opposition in Eastern Europe:
The Czechoslovak Example, London, 1976

A. Pravda, Reform and Change in the Czechoslovak
System, London, 1975

M. Rechcigl (ed.), The Czechoslovak Contribution to
World Culture, The Hague, 1964

H. Ripka, Czechoslovakia Enslaved, London, 1950

D. H. Schmidt, Anatomy of a Satellite, Boston, 1950

H. Gordon Skilling, Czechoslovakia's Interrupted
Revolution, Princeton, 1976

H. Schwartz, Prague's 200 Days, New York, 1969

R. Selucky, Czechoslovakia: The Plan That Failed,
London, 1970

W. Shawcross, Dubcek, London, 1970

O. Sik, Czechoslovakia. The Bureaucratic Economy,
New York, 1972

J. Slanska, Report on my Husband, London, 1969

M. Slingova, Truth Will Prevail, London, 1968

Z. Suda, The Czechoslovak Socialist Republic,
Baltimore, 1969

I. Svitak, The Czechoslovak Experiment, 1968-69,
New York, 1971

T. Szulc, Czechoslovakia Since World War II, New
York, 1971

E. Taborsky, Communism in Czechoslovakia, 1948-
1960, Princeton, 1961

P. Tigrid, Why Dubcek Fell, London, 1971

O. Ulc, Politics in Czechoslovakia, San Francisco, 1973

L. Vesely, Dubcek, Munich, 1970

W. V. Wallace, Czechoslovakia: Modern History, London, 1974

J. Wechsberg, The Voices, New York, 1969

K. Weisskopf, The Agony of Czechoslovakia, 1938-1968, London, 1968

G. W. Wheeler, The Human Face of Socialism, New York, 1973

P. Windsor & A. Roberts, Czechoslovakia 1968, Reform, Repression and Resistance, London, 1969

I. W. Zartman (ed.), Czechoslovakia: Intervention and Impact, New York, 1973

Z. A. B. Zeman, Prague Spring, London, 1968

P. E. Zinner, Communist Strategy and Tactics in Czechoslovakia, 1918-1948, London, 1963